SUPER CHILD!

Unlocking the Secrets of
Working Memory

Gayatri Kalra Sehgal

RUPA

Published by
Rupa Publications India Pvt. Ltd 2018
7/16, Ansari Road, Daryaganj
New Delhi 110002

Sales Centres:

Allahabad Bengaluru Chennai
Hyderabad Jaipur Kathmandu
Kolkata Mumbai

ISBN: 978-93-5333-305-8

First impression 2018

10 9 8 7 6 5 4 3 2 1

The moral right of the author has been asserted.

Printed at HT Media Ltd, Gr. Noida

To my sons,
Divyamshu and Kuber

Contents

KNOWLEDGE

PERCEPTION

CREATIVITY

Introduction

The Difficult Part: Forgetting

It is easier to remember than to forget!

Surprised?

Give it a try!

Try to forget something you remember!

Here is why: Children are born with a substantial capacity to retain information. As a child grows, he or she experiences and receives new information. With the new information and the knowledge already present in the memory, he or she begins to form 'associations'. As the child continues to acquire knowledge, he or she begins to build patterns of associations. These patterns get repeated again and again and become increasingly unintentional. They get stored in the nerve pathway of the brain as memory. To memorize things, it is essential to provide a learning environment conducive to the brain to form patterns of associations that get stored in the long-term memory for use when required. Similarly, to forget what we remember, we need to break these patterns of associations and create a roadblock in the nerve pathway, where the memory is stored. So, isn't forgetting more difficult than remembering?

Let us understand 'associations' with an example. Have you ever heard someone say, 'I cannot remember where I had kept my spectacles; I have a bad memory!' They then try to remember where they had been sitting last to read the newspaper. The very next moment, they remember where they had kept their spectacles! This entire journey of thought represents a 'pattern of associations'. In order to find the spectacles, one has to begin associating the sequence of events in the reverse order. Memory begins to jog, the mind then associates the sequence of events and is finally able to recall. We can recall things and events because we have associated a new memory with many other pre-existing memories. In this example, the person under consideration has associated the pre-existing memory of 'reading the newspaper' in the reverse order—where the person had been sitting and reading the newspaper to recalling what was lost—the spectacles!

What is a 'bad' memory or, as a matter of 'fact', what is a 'good' memory?

It is a myth!

The truth about 'memory' is: Either the memory is 'trained' or 'untrained'.

Trained memory is like a well-trodden path, where knowledge has travelled so many times that the response to knowledge becomes predictable and involuntary. The more the memory is trained, the better becomes the ability to recall. Now, how do we train the memory to recall?

Tip! The best way to train 'memory recall' is by increasing the attention in the 'memory forming' stage so that the information is stored well, to begin with.

We know this intuitively that if the child is interested in an activity, he or she will be able to absorb more information about the subject at hand. But, what we don't inspect is that, if the child is interested in an activity, the matrix of associations grows rapidly and becomes more permanent in the memory, and hence, the child is able to recall the information with ease.

All of us use our senses to absorb information. Out of the five senses, each of us uses a predominant sense to absorb maximum information. The information absorbed travels to the part of the brain called hippocampus. It is here that the information is simplified and the decisions are made—if the piece of information is worthy of being stored in the permanent long-term memory. The sensory information the senses absorb becomes permanent when the child pays attention to the information and observes it carefully.

Now, the question arises: How do we ensure that the child pays attention and 'observes' the information at the 'memory forming' stage?

If the answer to this is—by providing toys and games that you think will make the child learn and pay attention to internalize information—I would suggest you think again!

On the other hand, if, as facilitators and parents, you understand 'how' the child prefers to acquire information, would you still buy him or her the same toys and games?

'Learning styles' refer to the different ways children (people) learn to process and store information in their brain. Each child has a 'preferred learning style' that is his or her preferred way of absorbing information. Children gravitate towards their preferred learning style. For example, an auditory learner needs audio stimulation, such as verbal instructions, to learn and a visual learner requires a visually stimulating environment, such as diagrams. On the other hand, a logical learner requires enough reason to understand process and absorb information. To enhance learning, we need to tickle the preferred learning style of the child and then focus on the learning outcome. This way, the child will absorb information that he or she experiences naturally.

There are eight types of learning styles:

1. Auditory
2. Visual
3. Physical
4. Verbal
5. Social
6. Solitary
7. Logical
8. Naturalistic

Unfortunately, educators today offer information in limited learning styles. The teachers or educators, too, are not trained to cater to various kinds of learning styles. They instruct students in their preferred style of learning without realizing that it might not be the learning style suitable for the student who is absorbing the information. The facilitator might use a mix of audio and visual learning styles, whereas, the student may respond better to a subtle mix of naturalistic and solitary style.

The pressing need of the hour is to facilitate the child to consciously observe the information in the surroundings such that the child is able to form patterns of associations that result in forming the thinking patterns called 'perceptions' and are stored in their long-term memory.

To perceive is the ability to become aware or conscious about the knowledge around you through the senses. Perception, therefore, is the ability of how one perceives this knowledge.

How we perceive knowledge forms the base of our Intelligence Quotient (IQ). The IQ tests and scores are said to assess human intelligence. The aggregate score of these tests is derived from several standardized tests. However, IQ tests and scores are debatable. Therefore, it is best to not limit the child's ability solely based on these scores. Many times, children who did not score well in IQ tests or were assessed to have average intelligence, were seen doing well later in life!

Why so? It is because:

Tip! Memory is an ability that can be developed, but it requires mental effort, consistency and focused practice.

To excel in any sphere of life, the child needs to be able to form associations with new information and recall the memory when required. However, when he or she is unable to recall it at the right time, the child, despite being capable, shows negligible results. So, the question arises: *What is that **one superpower** that helps students excel in life, not just academically?* For the child to sustain in this competitive world, we need to facilitate him or her with not just memory and recall but help them manipulate information in a way that they can reformulate and use information when required. We need to help the child with his or her 'working memory' that commits to the long-term memory to work when required. Long-term memory is like a library of books in the brain and the working memory helps to identify and pull out a particular book whenever needed, reuse the information stored in it, form new associations, add more pages of information acquired, and place it back.

Tip! IQ is the knowledge you have and 'working memory' is how you can put that knowledge to use.

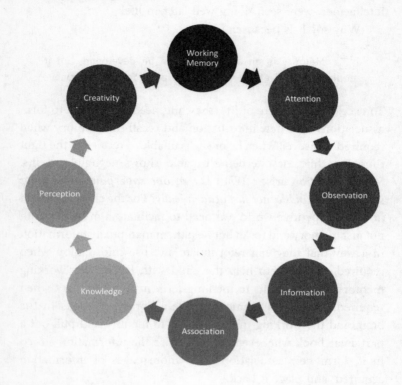

Working Memory Wheel

Not Just Memory but Working Memory

To facilitate children succeed in the world that is changing at a rapid pace, we need to keep abreast with the trends. The challenges we face today will not be the same as our emerging generations will be facing. However, without knowing the changes that the future is going to bring in, it becomes imperative for educators and parents to help children focus on their 'working memory' regardless of whether the child is neuro-typical* or has special needs.

We need to prepare children to be global leaders of tomorrow by enhancing the working memory at the right age. Unfortunately, the skills that should be enhanced to nurture children's future buckles under academic pressures and narrows down the possibility for them to evolve. We, as parents, need to make our children 'time-proof' and 'future-ready' by enhancing their working memory today. The anchor points of this memory serves as an **equalizer** and business leaders are on the lookout for them in potential candidates. Let us equate what 'working memory' offers and the requirements of business leaders in candidates.

Equalizer for Future Global Leaders

Anchor Points of Working Memory	Requirements of Business Leaders
Responsibility	Responsible
Decision-making	Decision-making
Leadership skills	Leadership skills
Team work	Team work
Punctuality	Time management
Attention	Focus
Understand knowledge	Manage information
Self-motivated	Go-getters
Associate	Network
Problem-solvers	Solve problems
Good behaviour	Strong work ethics

---

*Neuro-typical children fall in the average spectrum of development milestones-children who are not diagnosed with any intellectual or developmental difference and are intellectually, cognitively, and developmentally typical.

Risk-takers	Risk-takers
Explore and reformulate information	Research
Create	Innovate
Transition time	Manage change effectively
Manage stress	Manage stress
Confidence	Confidence

Now the question arises: How can we facilitate the child to achieve these goals? Mentioned below are the areas where a child uses his or her working memory to participate in everyday activities seriously. We need to have focused areas where we want to work with the child from the time when he or she is young and developing.

Where do School Children Use Working Memory?

Here are the areas where the child uses 'working memory' in day-to-day activities:

- Responding appropriately during a conversation
- Carrying out instructions that are age-appropriate
- Reading a newly-introduced or unknown word
- Paraphrasing spoken information (e.g., when the child conveys the meaning of something he or she had read or heard using a different set of words)
- Answering questions and recalling what to say when it's their turn to talk in class
- Daily organization
- Doing math in their minds
- Problem-solving skills
- Solving comprehension exercises

Golden rules

Nowadays, a lot of information is available at the click of a button, and an array of activities that parents and facilitators can engage their children in just by opening a screen. However, there are two golden rules for any activity we help the child with.

1. Remember, speed does not matter; forward is forward!

Whatever we do to help the child, we need to remember that every child has a learning pace and it can be optimized without comparing it with that of others. Facilitators and parents need to be positive and patient with the child. You need to help your child in the learning process. You must be open to learning and match your learning pace to that of the child's rather than expecting the child to match your teaching pace. Every positive step taken towards the target is a step forward. Keep moving forward with consistency and in the process, the pace will develop.

2. We work from strengths to weaknesses!

To begin with, identify a well-developed interest (or skill) of the child—a task which the child finds interesting and easy to do. Gradually, make the function of the task more and more challenging towards its completion. For example, if the child is fond of listening to stories and shows little interest in numeracy, we can choose a story of the child's interest that includes numeracy at a much easier level. In this way, we can use the strength of the child, which is listening to stories, and keep his or her interest alive, enhancing the not-so dominant interest (numeracy).

Cheat Sheet to Identify the Challenges

How can one identify if the child has working memory difficulties and requires your timely guidance?

Given below is 'the easy to identify tips' cheat sheet for parents and educators to notice clear indications in the child with difficulties with working memory. The child may demonstrate some traits while the others may remain unidentified at the moment. However, as informed facilitators, we need to identify and enhance the skills of the child by beginning from the child's present level of understanding. Take a pen and mark the answers that are true for your child.

If the child,

- demonstrates inadequate academic performance or shows slow progress despite working really hard. You will notice that it is not that the child is not putting in the required effort but is unable to hold on to information long enough to reformulate and process it.
- misses details in the instructions given to him or her.
- finds it difficult to organize or complete a task with multiple-step commands which is age appropriate. He or she might also find it difficult to start or complete their work independently; the child may rely on a bench partner in the classroom to be reminded about the current task.
- frequently makes mistakes in writing and counting in the classroom.
- fails to self-correct the work done in the classroom.
- gets easily distracted when he or she is not highly interested in an activity.
- finds it difficult to wait for their turn and interrupts the class or asks questions and then forgets what to say when called upon.
- misplaces belongings easily.
- shows below-average to average language abilities.
- finds it difficult to read, struggles to break sounds down

in words, is unable to blend the sounds into the word accurately, finds it difficult to keep track of his or her progress while reading and struggles with contextual cues to support word prediction.

- finds mental math difficult.
- finds problem-solving challenging.

How Can We Enhance Working Memory In Children?

To strengthen the working memory in a child, we need to take him or her through intensive training in this area. Training within specific activities has been proven to increase working memory. However, this is still an area for further research. It is important to note, however, that improving working memory through specific working memory-training activities can be a lengthy process. It might also require the task to be done frequently and repeat them to get the desired results.

Strengthening strategies

1. *Calculated Distractions*: Reduce background noise and distractions. Help the child to maintain attention long enough to process the information required to complete a task. Reducing distractions lessens the amount of information the child has to process. As the child masters the activity, you need to induce calculated distractions. Let us understand what calculated distractions are with an example.

   When the child has mastered an activity and can perform it without much effort, introduce distractions in the environment such as soft music. This will create just the correct amount of distraction, which the child will be able to ignore. When we introduce such calculated distractions in the child's learning environment, he or she begins to make extra efforts to concentrate on the subject of interest.

Gradually, increase the volume of the noise or distraction in the environment. The child will strive even harder to focus. Build on this trait to enhance concentration. Later, when the child needs to focus, for example, during the exams where the noise level is minimum or controlled, he or she will be able to ignore minor distractions without much effort. Remember to use the interest of the child to your benefit!

2. *Create and Establish Structure*: Children feel secure in a predictable environment. For example, if books or blankets are kept at the same place each time, and a child looks for his or her belongings, they feel comfortable and secured to predict their respective places in the house or at school. On the contrary, change in the environment disrupts focus. Build routines, structure and familiarity in activities as it helps to lessen the amount of new information the child has to absorb and process.

3. *Achieve Smaller Goals*: Break large and complex goals into smaller ones. Simplify information in a way that the child is able to understand and execute the instructions.

4. *Be Goal Specific*: As an educator or a parent, be clear about what you are assessing and focus on the target at hand rather than multiple targets at once. For example, while conducting a spelling test, focus on spellings only rather than letter formation, and handwriting.

5. *Slow the Pace*: While the child is motivated to take up more challenging activities, slow the pace of imparting instructions and information down. Allow the child adequate time to process the information and complete the activity.

6. *Effective Communication*: Communicate with the child as

much as possible and wait for the child to respond. Listen to the child. Do not be in a hurry; slow down the pace of delivery of information.

- Do not give long and non-sequential instructions, which sound confusing to the child.
- Use simple and clear language.
- Repeat specific language when you are making requests.
- If necessary, demonstrate what you want him or her to do.
- When you are giving an instruction to the child, encourage them to restate the given instruction back to you to ensure that the child has grasped or comprehended what is expected.

7. *Eye Contact*: Get close to the child to ensure that they are able to hear you and see your face. Get to their physical level to form an eye contact.

8. *Activities*: Complete repetitions of new activities ensure that the child has mastered the task. A child who is struggling with working memory will require more repetitions to learn a new task than others.

9. *Association*: Help the child to connect information to emotions and things he or she already knows. It helps them remember things easily.

10. *Engage All the Senses*: To help the child make the required information more permanent in the long-term memory, present it to him or her in a multi-sensorial manner. Use their preferred learning style to help them imbibe information. For example, have your child type multiplication tables in different fonts, sing them aloud, listen to their peer say the table and do a craft activity using different materials like sand, etc.

11. *Record Book*: Create a working memory record book with the child of important information he or she can utilize at home or in the classroom.

12. *Classroom Strategies*: Reinforce with the child that it is okay to ask for help or repetitions of information. Pair the child with a friend, give them instructions and let them share the load to complete tasks.

13. *Visualize*:
    • Encourage the child to visualize what he or she hears.
    • Use visuals and gestures to help the child remember steps involved in a task such as a morning routine.
    • Encourage the child to write verbal information down or draw a picture. They can click photographs of important things they may need to remember.
    • During the activity, draw the information you want the child to remember. Talk about the information in the drawing. Allow the child adequate time to look at the drawing and the information provided by you. Next, ask the child to close his or her eyes and imagine the drawing. Ask what he or she can see, read, smell and feel while the eyes are still closed.

14. *Stay Calm*: Stress and anxiety at any age reduces the capacity of working memory significantly. Teach the child self-calming techniques when they feel stressed. Also, as a facilitator, maintain your calm as your reaction on the child's efforts will impact his or her self-esteem, -confidence and -image.

15. *Consult a Child Development Specialist*: Take the child to a specialist to rule out any possible underlying concerns and to probe working memory issues at the earliest. Professional

advice is better at an earlier stage than at an advanced stage when the child's development is delayed and he or she is physically more mature.

Remember to Remember

1. *Resources*: This book contains a short list of materials that you will need before you begin the activity. More often than not, these are everyday household items you might already have. Save junk, as many activities in this book will require recyclable material. Other materials may need to be purchased from craft shops or local stationery stores.

2. *Gadgets*: Turn off the computer, TV and spend quality time with your child working on the activities in this book. This will contribute to the child's development and stand them a good stead in the years to come.

3. *Holistic Development*: These activities will encourage the enthusiastic learners to absorb, associate and reformulate recent information to develop their long-term memory and speed up their holistic development.

4. *Focused Skill Development*: The goals that can be achieved have been provided with each activity to help facilitators develop focused skills with the child.

5. *Compliment Every Improvement*: On the first day, record the number of accurate answers given by the child so that you can complement him or her for every improvement.

6. *Level of Complexity*: To begin with, keep things simple and easy for the child to gain confidence. Do not increase the level of complexity too early.

7. *Indication of Mastery*: Keep a stopwatch handy, as most of

the activities will require to be timed. The time taken to complete the activity with accuracy indicates how far the child has mastered an activity.

8. *Communication*: As memory is not a toy or tangible, which a child could hold or play with, training his or her working memory will require lots of open-ended conversations with family and friends. Make a note of his or her daily interests and creatively weave them into your daily conversations.

9. *Disagree to Form Opinions*: Allow the child to think, disagree and debate, as this will help him or her form opinions.

10. *Starting Points for Comparison*: Assess the child's capabilities from the point where you started as a team, and compare his or her development as you progress rather than in comparison to other children.

11. *Support the Child*: The book will help you discover those areas of learning that your child needs to build upon and may require extra time. Every child develops at his or her pace, and parents can help optimize it. Support the child to develop a healthy self-image with lots of encouragement, quality time and love.

12. *Learning Environment*: In the activities the word 'child' has been used interchangeably as a 'player' or 'chef'. Use it to create the serious and boring learning environment into an enjoyable and stress-free one.

13. *Hear from the Bosses*: While some activities require adult participation, others merely require a parent's guidance to convince the child to get started. The activities in this book are only starters! We would love to hear from you, how you and your child evolved during the activities, and

which activities you enjoyed the most. Remember to add and change whatever you want.

You and your children are the boss!

Don't forget to create fond memories during the memory workouts!

My name is_____

This is me!

Attention!

Activity 1

Attention!

Players: 2 to 3

Getting Ready:

1. Take a printed (not handwritten) story, keeping the current reading level of the child in mind.
2. Take a printout of one paragraph or 4–5 lines from the story in the same font.

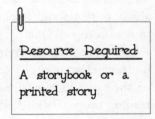

Resource Required:

A storybook or a printed story

3. Keep the fonts simple in the beginning, and later, try to use more complex fonts that require more concentration while reading.
4. The printed text of the story should have 2–3 different, yet simple, fonts such as Arial, Times New Roman (school teachers generally use this font) or Comic Sans.

How to Play:

1. Give the child the printed text to read.
2. Allow him or her adequate time to read the text.
3. Start the stopwatch and note the time taken by him or her to read each paragraph.

Tickle the Thoughts

After the child has finished reading the paragraphs of the story, ask 2–3 questions per paragraph that the child has read.

Suggestions:

1. Note how many questions per paragraph the child is able to answer.
2. Check the complexity level of the font used, the time taken to read the paragraph and the number of accurate answers given by the child.

NOTE: Some children learn better when they have to focus more on complex fonts. Research suggests that children have a better ability to retain and respond when they have to put extra effort to read complex fonts.

However, all children respond differently. Therefore, first, understand your child's capabilities. Check how much time he or she takes to learn when complex fonts are used and while reading the text with fonts as simple as Comic Sans. The idea is to enhance the attention span in order to get the best results.

Goals Achieved:
- Attention
- Enhanced reading skills
- Retention of information

TICK-TACK TIP

Do not over-complicate the font. Keep the fonts legible.

Activity 2

Missing Objects!

Players: 2 to 3

Getting Ready:

1. Keep 5–8 objects such as a book, toy, crayons, glue and an apple etc., on a tray.
2. A stopwatch

> **Resources Required:**
> 1. Five to eight different common objects such as, book, crayons, glue, apple, toy, a tray.
> 2. A stopwatch

How to Play:

1. Place the objects on the tray.
2. Set the stopwatch for 1 minute. Then, display the objects in front of the child.
3. Invite the child to observe or study the objects for a minute.
4. After a minute, remove or cover the tray.
5. Remove an object from the tray and show the tray again to the child for 30 seconds.

Tickle the Thoughts:

1. Ask your child how many objects were there on the tray when he or she saw it for the first time.
2. Name the object that was removed from the tray.
3. Name the tasty object on the plate.

🎯 Goals Achieved:
- Attention
- Observation
- Thinking skills

TICK-TACK TIPS

1. As the players learn the tricks, increase the complexity of the game by increasing the number of objects kept on the tray and reducing the number of missing objects. At times, do not remove anything at all from the tray!

2. Reduce the time given to the child to observe the objects.

3. Place numerous objects on the tray and remove only one or two things from it. Also, do not increase the size of the tray.

Activity 3

Schultz Table!

Players: 2 to 3

Getting Ready:

1. Take a few A4-sized papers, 3–4 coloured felt pens and a ruler.

2. Set the timer for 25–30 seconds on the stopwatch.

> **Resources Required:**
>
> 1. Papers of A4 size, colour felt pens, scale, stopwatch
> 2. A coloured print of the given table

3. Take a printout or a handwritten 5×5 Schultz table with numbers written in different colours.

How to Make More Schultz Table:

1. Draw a table with five columns and five rows.

2. Write a number at the centre of the table at the 'sight fixate point' like the number 18 in the table given below.
   (Sight fixate point is the point on the sheet where the child has to fix his or her sight before they begin their search for the numbers visually).

3. Write the numbers in the grid beginning from 1 to 25 in a random manner.

4. Ensure that the numbers are not written sequentially in one horizontal row, as the horizontal eye movement is not allowed.

5. Use not more than three to four coloured felt pens to write the numbers in the grid.

How to Play:

1. Ask the player to focus at the centre 'fixate point' of the grid (number 18).
2. Ask the player to find all the numbers starting from 1 in ascending order.
3. Ask the player not to move the hands to point out the numbers; the idea is to increase the field of vision.
4. Invite the other player to watch the movement of the hands, head and eyes of the first player.
5. The player who moves the hands or the head is eliminated.
6. Start the time and ask the child to start finding and counting the numbers in ascending order.
7. Ensure that the entire table is clearly visible to the player.
8. The distance between the table and the eye remains the same throughout, which is approximately 25 to 30 cm.
9. Help the child to fixate the sight at the centre of the table; in the given example, it is at number 18 in the table.
10. Next, ask the player to search for the numbers beginning from number 1 in the ascending order.
11. Start the timer of the stopwatch for 30 seconds.

Tickle the Thoughts:

1. Was the time given to you challenging?
2. What were you thinking during the given time?

Schultz Table!

		Sight Fixate		

13	22	21	8	10
17	4	1	24	20
6	25	18	3	16
19	11	23	9	14
2	15	12	7	5

Goals Achieved:

- Enhance the child's field of vision—an essential instrument for speed reading.
- Enhance the rate of development—in particular, the speed of visual-search movements.
- Colour code enhances 'attention-switching' ability.
- Completion speed and the number of mistakes made are the measurement of their efficiency.

TICK-TACK TIPS

1. The increasing level of complexity would be to start by helping the child not move his or her hands to find the numbers, and he or she must keep the head still. The next level would be to not move the eyes.

2. The expansion of the field of vision can be reached accurately by following the rules of the tables regularly. The field of vision is the area that a person's or an animal's eye can see when it is fixed at one position (number 18) without moving the head.

3. Develop accuracy first and then speed.

4. Use a stopwatch to facilitate the child to develop the speed of one letter per second; the child should be able to identify 25 letters in 25 seconds or less. Lesser the time, greater is the reading speed!

5. You can make a table using letters too.

6. Fixing the eyes only at the centre of the table is authorised.

7. Horizontal movements of eyes are forbidden.

Activity 4

How Many Can You Name?

Players: 2 to 3

Getting Ready:

1. Keep small chits of paper ready with categories written on them.

How to Play:

1. Assign a number to all the players.
2. Invite the players to pick up a chit.
3. Ask them to open the chit and read the category and cite examples from the category mentioned.
4. Invite the other players to identify the category.

> **Resources Required:**
>
> 1. Undivided attention
> 2. Time
> 3. Small chits of paper with word categories written on them such as reptiles, dinosaurs, arctic animals, aquatic plants, mountains, deserts

Tickle the Thoughts:

Build upon the category of the child's choice. Ask him or her to share more information about the chosen categories. For example, if the chit reads 'mountains', ask questions such as—which is the highest mountain in the world? or why are mountains covered with snow?

Goals Achieved:
- Concentration
- Information bank
- Thinking skills
- Communication skills

TICK-TACK TIP

Reward the player for correct and precise answers with a year's subscription of informative children's magazines or a visit to a botanical garden.

Magic in the Cup!

Players: 2 to 3

Getting Ready:

1. Keep three cups, a coin and a scarf ready.

How to Play:

1. To add some fun to the activity, parents or facilitators can tie a scarf around their necks to resemble a magician.

Resources Required:
1. Three opaque cups
2. One small object such as a coin
3. A scarf or a bed sheet (optional)

2. Reverse the three cups and carefully place a coin under one of the cups; make sure the child knows under which cup the coin has been placed.
3. Ask the child to carefully observe as you move the cup with the coin under it.
4. To begin with, slowly drag and dodge the cups.
5. Then, increase the speed of moving the cups such that the child has to pay more attention to know under which cup the coin has been placed.
6. Your child can then have a go at transporting the magic cups.
7. Handover the magician's cape to your child and ask him or her to perform the trick.

Tickle the Thoughts:

As you move the cups around, ask your child which cup has the coin.

If the child gets the answer incorrect, ask him or her to check if the coin disappeared under the table or if it has magically travelled to their bags or if it is stuck in their sleeves.

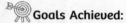

Goals Achieved:

- Concentration
- Role play
- Leadership skills

TICK-TACK TIP

Open-ended questions give parents the insight into the child's thoughts and fears.

Activity 6

Needle in the Haystack!

Players: 2 to 3

Getting Ready:

1. Keep a bale of straw, haystack, a carton and small-sized sweets ready.
2. A stopwatch.
3. An eye mask.

> **Resources Required:**
>
> 1. A bale of straw, haystack, a carton and small-sized sweets
> 2. A stopwatch
> 3. An eye mask

How to Play:

1. Blindfold the player using the eye mask.
2. Place the haystack or the bale of straw in the carton.
3. Hide the sweets in the hay.
4. Ask one player to start the timer.
5. Each player gets only 60 seconds to find as many sweets as possible.
6. The player who finds the most number of sweets in the allocated time is the winner.

Tickle the Thoughts:

1. How many sweets do you think were there in the carton?
2. Encourage all the players to count their set of sweets and invite the winner to count the total.

Goals Achieved:
- Concentration
- Sensory enhancement
- Numeracy

TICK-TACK TIPS

1. To significantly enhance the sensory skills, reduce the size of sweets and increase the quantity of haystack and the time for searching the sweets.

2. You can place small-sized toy animals in the haystack and ask the child to repeat the activity. Once the child finds the animals in the allocated time, ask them to identify the animals while their eyes are still covered with the eye mask.

School is Cool!

Players: 2 to 3

Getting Ready:

1. Create a story about going to school.

How to Play:

Resources Required:

1. A story about going to school
2. Time without limitations

1. Ask the child to imagine that he or she is going to school.
2. Assign a number to each player.
3. Start the game by saying, 'I will get up early to go to school.'
4. Then ask the next player, 'What will you do next?'
5. Ask the players not to repeat what the previous player said.

Tickle the Thoughts:

1. What was your sister's (player's name) number?
2. Why should we get up early or late to attend school?
3. What is the sequence of things you (the child) will require to do before attending school?
4. What will you do at school?
5. How will you come back from school?

Goals Achieved:
- Sequencing
- Concept of time, punctuality
- Attention
- Accuracy

TICK-TACK TIP

Open-ended questions give parents the insight into the child's thoughts and fears.

Spot the Difference I!

Players: 2 to 3

Getting Ready:

1. Wear a lot of clothes. For example, a shirt, handkerchief in the front pocket of the shirt, trousers, tie, shoes, socks, blazer and watch.
2. Set the stopwatch for one minute.

Resources Required:

1. A shirt, handkerchief in the front pocket of the shirt, trousers, tie, shoes, socks and a watch
2. A stopwatch

How to Play:

1. Invite the child to observe what you are wearing for one minute.
2. Leave the room, change one thing. Come back to the room and ask the child to spot the difference.
3. Give the child 30 seconds to spot the difference.

Tickle the Thoughts:

1. What all were you wearing before you left the room?
2. What did you change?
3. Would you (the child) like to change something for me to spot the difference?

Goals Achieved:
- Concentration
- Observation
- Eye for detail

TICK-TACK TIPS

1. To begin with, replace something that is big in size like a blazer; change into a shirt and gradually make the change smaller and more intricate such as, changing cufflinks or earrings!
2. Gradually reduce the time given to spot the number of differences.

Activity 9

Spot the Difference II!

Players: 2 to 3

Getting Ready:

1. Draw 8 to 10 objects on a piece of paper with a pencil.

How to Play:

1. Invite the player to observe the drawing for one minute.
2. Erase a few objects on the paper.
3. Ask the player to spot the missing objects.

Resources Required:

1. A paper
2. A pencil
3. An eraser

Tickle the Thoughts:

1. What were the 10 things drawn on the paper?
2. What was erased?
3. Ask them if they would like to take the lead in the game and draw.

Goals Achieved:

- Concentration
- Eye for detail
- Drawing skills
- Fine motor skills

TICK-TACK TIPS

1. Draw the things that the player is familiar with and can name.
2. If the child finds it difficult to draw, you can use objects or toys.
3. Gradually reduce the time given to spot the difference with the increased number of differences.

Activity 10

Rhyming Words!

Players: 2 to 3

Getting Ready:

1. Pre-cut an A4-sized sheet of paper into small eight to ten chits.
2. On each chit, draw or write the first rhyming word.

How to Play:

Resources Required:

1. A paper
2. A pencil
3. An eraser
4. A list of age-appropriate rhyming words

1. Assign each player a number.
2. Invite the first player to begin the game by giving the first word from the chit.
3. Ask another player to give another rhyming word.
4. Urge the players not to repeat the word.

Tickle the Thoughts:

1. What was the rhyming word player number 2 had given?
2. What was the rhyming word given by you?
3. The player who repeats the word is eliminated.

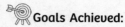

Goals Achieved:
- Concentration
- Sequencing
- Vocabulary enhancement
- Rhyme recognition
- Recognition of phonemic changes in words

TICK-TACK TIP

If the player does not completely understand the concept of rhyming words, introduce the game by giving the player a set of rhyming words. Include one word that does not rhyme with the given set of words. Invite the player to identify the odd word out.

Activity 11

Shop Till You Drop!

Players: 2 to 3

Getting Ready:

1. Make up a story about going to the market to buy groceries.

How to Play:

1. Invite the child to imagine that you all are going to the market to buy groceries.
2. Assign a number to each player.
3. Introduce the game by saying, 'I will get ready and pick up the car keys.'
4. Then, enquire from the neighbouring player: What will you do next?
5. Ask the child not to repeat what has already been said.
6. Ask the players what groceries do they require everyday.

Resources Required:

1. A story about going to the market to buy groceries
2. Unlimited time

Tickle the Thoughts:

1. What was the number assigned to your friend (player's name)?
2. What did you do before going to the grocery store?
3. Ask for the sequence of events for putting the groceries in the trolley and then reverse the sequence of events to increase the complexity.

4. What would you like to buy the next time you go to the grocery store?

🎯 Goals Achieved:
- Sequencing
- Attention
- Accuracy

TICK-TACK TIP

Open-ended questions give parents the insight into the child's mind.

Observation

Activity 12

Memory Palace!

Players: 2 to 3

Getting Ready:

1. Take out some time for a walk in your 'palace'.

Resources Required:

1. A list of 10 things
2. A walk in the house

How to Play:

1. Ask the child to make a list of 10 things he or she usually forgets to take to school such as, a lunchbox, identity card, notebooks, and a handkerchief.
2. Facilitate the child to carefully plan a route through the house—the palace—such that the child identifies and remembers the particular locations in the room, also called peg points.
3. Ask the child to take a walk in the 'palace' and come back to you after completing the tour.
4. During the walk in each room, ask the child to associate the objects in the list with specific locations or peg points.
5. The child can choose one peg point or ten peg points per room; it does not matter as long as each peg point is distinct and the child rehearses the journey without missing the peg points.
6. Ask the child to visualize the item on the list with the particular peg point. For example, if the object on the list

is a lunchbox and the location or peg point is the dining table, then ask the child to visualize the table eating the food in the lunchbox and then burping loudly.

7. The human brain likes to have fun! Bizarre images are easier to memorize. Remember to associate peg points and the objects with some element of fun.

Tickle the Thoughts:

1. Now, ask the child if he or she can take the same journey in his or her mind rather than actually taking the route.

Check list: If the child misses peg points and changes the route, it will indicate that the peg points and the visual interaction of the objects with the peg points were not established properly.

Goals Achieved:
- Visual-spatial memory
- Enhanced three-dimensional memory

TICK-TACK TIPS

1. Remember to establish a strong link, which is also funny, between the objects in the list and peg points.
2. Try to give a list of grocery items to the child.
3. Before leaving for shopping, ask the child to mentally identify peg points, and during shopping, ask the child to tell you the items. Ask the child to retrace the journey without missing any peg point.

Observation Perfected!

Players: 2 to 3

Getting Ready:

1. Remember to take a closer look at a place where everyone was sitting a short while ago.

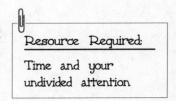

Resource Required:

Time and your undivided attention

How to Play:

1. Ask a child to describe the room they were sitting in without looking back into the room.
2. Ask the child to describe the room in detail.

Tickle the Thoughts:

1. How many items were there?
2. What was the colour of specific items?
3. Name the number of items present in the room.
4. Ask the location of items such as laptop, mobile phones, etc.
5. How many doors, windows and furniture were there in the room?

Goals Achieved:

- Observation skills
- Visual memory recall

TICK-TACK TIP

As the child develops observation skills, go outdoors like bird sanctuaries, art museums, botanical gardens, etc., where he or she gets to see different kinds of birds, trees, art forms and later remember to discuss their observations.

Activity 14

Snaps and Claps

Players: 2 to 3

Getting Ready:

1. Create sounds by tapping on the table, snapping fingers or by clapping hands.

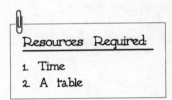

Resources Required:

1. Time
2. A table

How to Play:

1. Create a sound in a particular pattern by clapping.
2. Invite the child to listen carefully for any variation in the sound.
3. Ask him or her to identify the 'missed beat' by telling you to 'stop'.
4. Ask the player to repeat the beats.

Tickle the Thoughts:

1. Ask the child to propose how else can he or she create a sound.
2. Encourage them to think about tapping their thighs or the table.

Goals Achieved:

- Concentration
- Listening skills

- Audio-kinaesthetic coordination
- Sound recognition

TICK-TACK TIP

Include variation by missing more beats for a briefer interval for the child to identify.

Magic Mats!

Players: 5 to 6

Getting Ready:

1. Keep two identical sets of eight to ten objects or toys such as toy insects, two trays and a few napkins to cover ready.

> **Resource Required:**
>
> Two identical sets of eight to ten objects or toys such as insects, two trays, few napkins to cover

How to Play:

1. Ask one player to place five to six toy insects in a particular manner on a tray and show it to the next player only for 30 seconds.
2. Invite the second player to observe the toy insects.
3. Ask the first player to remove the insects from the tray.
4. Next, ask the second player to place the insects on the tray exactly in the same manner the first player had shown.

Tickle the Thoughts:

1. Do you remember the number of insects?
2. How far were they placed from each other?
3. Was the 'caterpillar' facing left or right?

Goals Achieved:

- Visual-spatial analysis of information
- Exercises the short-term memory

TICK-TACK TIPS

1. Add plenty of insects to the same tray such that the tray is full of insects and reduce the time given for observation.
2. Mix toy insects with other toys such as toy reptiles.
3. Keep some toys upside down.

Activity 16

Chocolates—All for Me!

Players: 2 to 3

Getting Ready:

Keep molten chocolate in a small bowl, oversized clothes, dice, six child-safe forks, a well-set table with plates and table napkins ready.

Resources Required:
1. Molten chocolate in a small dish
2. Oversized unisex clothes
3. A dice
4. 6 Child-safe forks
5. A well-set table with plates and table napkins

How to Play:

1. Assign a number to all the players.
2. Ask a player to wear the dress and roll the dice.
3. Ask the player to guess the number on the dice without counting the dots on them.
4. Ask the child to take his or her fork to gulp down the melted chocolate.
5. The player who drops the chocolate on the table should be eliminated from the game.

Tickle the Thoughts:

1. Build upon the child's table manners.
2. The player who does not drop any chocolate wins the game.

3. Ask the players about the importance of being clean and good table manners.

🎯 **Goals Achieved:**
- Concentration
- Table etiquettes
- Cleanliness
- Numeracy

TICK-TACK TIPS

1. You can introduce table manners in a fun way as the melted chocolate tends to spill everywhere! Children enjoy the 'messy' chocolates.
2. To increase the level of complexity, melt the chocolate and reduce the size of the dish.
3. Encourage the players to talk about the importance of good table manners.

Activity 17

Card-2-Card!

Players: 2 to 3

Getting Ready:

1. Choose a time of the day when there is not much disturbance in the surroundings.

2. Keep two packs of standard playing cards ready.

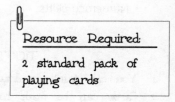

Resource Required:

2 standard pack of playing cards

How to Play:

1. Collect two packs of cards; pull out a set of four to five identical pairs of cards.

2. Shuffle the cards and place the set of cards face-down on the table in 4–5 rows.

3. Invite each player to find an identical pair by turning up two cards.

4. If it is not a matching pair, then the player places the cards facing down again in the same position.

5. If the pair match, the player keeps the pair of cards and gets a bonus turn.

6. When all the pairs have been found, players count their pairs.

7. The one with the most pair of cards is the winner.

Tickle the Thoughts:

1. Ask the child where did they see the identical match of the chosen card.
2. Tell them to count the number of pairs they have.

Goals Achieved:
- Concentration
- Visual recognition
- Numeracy skills

TICK-TACK TIPS

1. You can paint or draw the cards at home.
2. Cards can be made to facilitate the child to learn specific things such as pictures of the Seven Wonders of the World on the cards and the child has to find that particular wonder's details on the other card.

Activity 18

Coins on the Table, Coins on My Mind!

Players: 2 to 3

Getting Ready:

1. Choose a time of the day when the surroundings are relatively quieter.
2. Keep 10–15 coins, a flat surface such as a table or tray, stopwatch and camera ready.

> **Resources Required:**
>
> 1. 10 to 15 coins
> 2. Horizontal surfaces such as a table or a tray
> 3. A stopwatch
> 4. A camera

How to Play:

1. Collect the coins and place them in a random order of heads and tails.
2. Allow the child to observe the coins for a minute.
3. Then, remove the coins and hand them over to your child.
4. Click the picture of the coins to match the answers given by the players later.
5. Ask the child to arrange the coins in the same order.

Tickle the Thoughts:

1. Ask the child to guess the total number of coins placed.
2. Ask the child how many coins were placed with heads facing down.
3. Ask him or her how many tails could he or she see.

🎯 **Goals Achieved:**
- Observation
- Concentration
- Visual recognition
- Numeracy skills

TICK-TACK TIP

You may complicate this game by using different currencies.

Hurray, Hurray It's a Holi-Holiday!

Players: 2 to 3

Getting Ready:

1. Make up a fun-filled story about going on a holiday.

How to Play:

1. Ask the players to imagine that the whole family is going on a holiday.

> **Resources Required:**
> 1. A story about going on a holiday
> 2. Some extra time to spare.

2. Assign a number to each player.
3. Start the game by saying, 'I packed my bag, and put a toothbrush inside it.'
4. Then invite the next player to add one more thing to the bag.
5. Ask the child not to repeat what has already been put in the bag.

Tickle the Thoughts:

1. What was your friend's (player's name) number?
2. Which object was placed after my toothbrush in the bag?
3. Ask the sequence of putting the objects in the bag.
4. What else would you like to carry in your bag?

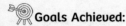

Goals Achieved:
- Attention
- Sequencing
- Attention
- Accuracy

TICK-TACK TIP

Open-ended questions give parents the insight into a child's mind. Keep asking questions to the young genius.

Activity 20

We're Going to the Zoo...o...o!

Players: 2 to 3

Getting Ready:

1. Arrange a trip to the nearby zoo and remember to carry a camera.
2. Have a video recorder ready as well.

> Resources Required:
>
> 1. A visit to the zoo
> 2. A video recorder
> 3. A camera
> 4. Two to three players

How to Play:

1. Explore the zoo with the children.
2. Ask the child to listen carefully to the sounds the animals and birds make.
3. Invite the children one by one to video record the sounds of various birds and animals.
4. Ask the children to photograph the birds and animals too.

Tickle the Thoughts:

1. Once back home, show them the pictures of the birds and animals and ask them to imitate their cries one-by-one.
2. Share the videos of the birds and animals with the children and ask them if they had imitated their cries correctly!

🎯 Goals Achieved:
- Audio-visual memory
- Creativity
- Oral-motor skill development

TICK-TACK TIPS

1. Share information about birds and animals.
2. Help children to understand the camera and its features.

Activity 21

Off to the Zoo, How About You?

Players: 2 to 3

Getting Ready:

1. Arrange a trip to a nearby zoo and remember to include a camera, pre-cut printed pictures of the birds and animals and their homes.
2. Video recording of the previous trip to the zoo.

> **Resources Required:**
> 1. Pre-cut printed pictures of the birds and animals and their homes
> 2. A video of the trip to the zoo

How to Play:

1. Keep the printed pictures out of children's sight.
2. Now invite one child to imitate the sound of one of the animals they had seen at the zoo. Let's suppose that he or she has chosen to roar.
3. Ask the next child to identify the bird or animal that the first child imitates (in this case, a lion).
4. Share the pictures of the birds and animals. Let the child pick up an accurate picture of the animal or bird and place it in its correct home (in this case, den).

Tickle the Thoughts:

1. Share the pictures of various birds and animals and their homes with the children and ask them what they observed about those birds and animals.
2. What material is the child's home made of?
3. What do you think the birds and animals need to survive?
4. What do you (the child) need to survive?

Goals Achieved:

- Audio-visual memory
- Concept-building

TICK-TACK TIPS

1. Share information about different kinds of birds and animals and their homes using recyclable material.
2. Help children understand that animals, too, need shelter, food, water, love and care.
3. You might even consider subscribing children's magazines for the group.

Activity 22

Match the Names to Faces!

Players: 2 to 3

Getting Ready:

1. Keep a newspaper, safety scissors, glue, sheets of A4-sized papers ready.

> **Resource Required:**
>
> A newspaper, safety scissors, glue, sheets of A4-sized papers

How to Play:

1. Give the child the newspaper and scissors and ask him or her to cut the pictures of faces from the newspaper.
2. Ask him or her to observe at least one special feature of the person in the picture and allow them to be creative and funny.
3. Give some glue to the children and ask them to paste the pictures on the A4-sized sheets.
4. While they are pasting the pictures, talk to them about the person in the picture.
5. Once they have finished pasting the pictures, ask them to recall the names of the people.

Tickle the Thoughts

1. Find a word that rhymes with the name or a thought that reminds you of, for instance, 'Uncle Bose'.
2. What do you think about, 'Uncle Bose'? What is the first

thing that comes to your mind about him? (Children love to observe unusual physical features of people such as a big belly, large scary eyes, bushy eyebrows, big nose, etc.)

3. Ask the child to associate the two things.

Here is how:

'Uncle Bose' got a 'rose' and has a big 'nose'!

| Name (of the person to be remembered) | Rhyme (with an object) | Unusual feature |

Goals Achieved:
- Recall
- Observation
- Association

TICK-TACK TIPS

1. Repeat the activity until the child gets used to observing the unique features of a person and automatically relates them to his name.

2. Then move ahead from cut and paste activity to associating with people.

3. Encourage the child to name the new friend often during his or her conversation in order to remember the names of friends.

Information

Chunking Patterns!

Players: 2 to 3

Getting Ready:

1. Get handwritten or printed flashcards.
2. A stopwatch.

> **Resources Required:**
> 1. Flashcards (provided)
> 2. A stopwatch

How to Play:

1. Have a predetermined set of numbers, like phone numbers, written on different sheets.
2. Ask one player to show one sheet to the other player for 15 seconds and then remove it.
3. Ask the first player to announce the numbers in the exact sequence.
4. Maintain silence.

Tickle the Thoughts

1. Can you recollect the numbers in the correct sequence?
2. Can you recall your friend's cell number?

Variation 1

07031962

Now help the player by using the format of a date instead of the date: July, 3rd, 1962.

Furthermore, facilitate the child to associate the date with a person. In this case, it is Tom Cruise, and show this picture to the child.

Now show the child the same flashcard, ask the same question, and reflect on the results obtained.

Variation 2

7905905504

Repeat the rules of the game.

Try different sorts of 'association' techniques for different kinds of learners to help them memorize and store information.

Show them the flashcards and ask them to repeat the numbers in the correct sequence.

Now help them break down the numbers into more bite-sized chunks such as,

$$790\text{-}590\text{-}550\text{-}4$$

Easier, isn't it?

Furthermore, show the picture of your friend (the owner of the cell number) to the child and remind him or her of the strawberries that a friend had once brought! Here, you are helping the child to associate the numbers with the visual of the person and the taste of strawberries in his or her memory.

 Goals Achieved:
- Pattern recognition
- Problem-solving
- Enhanced ability to break down large and difficult-to-memorize information into more manageable and memorable chunks

---

TICK-TACK TIPS

1. Show the flashcard to the child for 15 seconds and ask him or her to say the numbers in correct sequence.
2. To begin with, start with a smaller sequence of numbers.
3. After the child has finished telling you the numbers, share the flashcards with the player.

Activity 24

Mind Mapping!

Players: 2 to 3

Getting Ready:

Keep a few sheets of paper, felt pens and markers for each child ready.

Resources Required:

A paper (A4-sized or bigger), felt pens, markers

How to Play:

1. Give the child different coloured felt pens and an A4-sized sheet, and ask him or her to hold it lengthwise, i.e., in landscape orientation.

2. Ask the child to choose a topic for discussion such as, picnic.

3. Ask the child to write or draw the image of the topic of discussion at the centre of the page.

4. As you begin to discuss about the 'picnic', ask the child to draw curved lines beginning from the word 'picnic'.

5. The curved lines should lead to the sub-headings. The sub-headings should be a single word that represents the thoughts of the child revolving around the topic 'picnic'.

6. Discuss the sub-headings with the child and allow the child to give information about the sub-headings. These sub-headings can be (LPPL) Location, Purpose, People, Logistics and so on.

7. Allow the child to have as many sub-headings as possible so long as the child is able to trace the journey back to the

centre when required. The lines can further narrow down to sub-subheadings.

8. Ask the child to give only one word for one thought process; avoid long confusing sentences.
9. Ask the child to draw images whenever possible.

Tickle the Thoughts:

1. Where do you want to go for a picnic?
2. What is the purpose of the picnic? Do you want to go on an educational or informative trip such as to a museum, or for fun?
3. Whom do you want to go with—school friends or with family?
4. How do you want to travel?

Goals Achieved:
- Network of associations
- Visual thinking
- Organization skills
- Clear thinking

TICK-TACK TIP

Mind maps are an effective way to organize visual thoughts to create a network of new associations with the already existing information.

Activity 25

Guess Who?

Players: 5 to 6

Getting Ready:

1. Have eight to ten pictures of a few notable people and a two-way stick-on tape ready.

How to Play:

1. Assign a number to each player.

2. Pin a famous name on the player's back and number the player. Keep the identity of the famous person hidden.

3. Then the player number one has to guess the identity of the famous person by asking questions such as:
   - Am I a female?
   - Do I play a game or star in movies?
   - Was I born in India?

4. Player number one can ask one player only one question.

5. The other players can give answers only in 'yes' or 'no.'

6. At the end of the game, the player who discovers the identity of the famous person with the least number of questions is the winner.

Resources Required:

1. Old recyclable magazines
2. A two-way stick-on tape
3. A pair of child-safe scissors

Goals Achieved:
- Recalling
- Reasoning
- Finding solutions
- Cognitive skills

TICK-TACK TIPS

1. To encourage the players, you can begin by using pictures of well-known relatives.
2. Instead of asking questions, ask the other players to mimic them.

Activity 26

Sink and Float!

Players: 2 to 3

Getting Ready:

1. Keep five objects that sink into the water ready.
2. Keep five objects that float on the water ready.
3. Get a tub full of water.

How to Play:

1. Assign numbers to all the players.
2. Give one object at a time to each player.

Resources Required:

1. Five objects that sink into the water such as a stone, an egg, a pen, coin and shell.
2. Five objects that float on the water such as a paper boat, a ball, dry leaves, balloons and oil.
3. A tub full of water.

Tickle the Thoughts:

1. Ask the players to pick up one object at a time.
2. Before the player puts the object into the water, ask him or her to guess if the object would sink or float, and why.

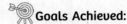

Goals Achieved:

- Concentration
- Information bank
- Thinking skills
- Concept-building

TICK-TACK TIP

Share facts about boats, ships, submarines, hovercrafts with the players to develop their information bank.

Activity 27

NPAT Game!

Players: 4 to 5

Getting Ready:

1. Fix one sheet of paper on a clipboard for each player.
2. Keep one pencil for each player ready.

> **Resources Required:**
>
> Papers, pencils and clipboards for all the players

How to Play:

1. Give each player a sheet and a pencil.
2. Assign a number to each player.
3. Ask the first player to choose a letter and read it out aloud. For example, the first player chooses the letter 'M'.
4. Ask each player to make four columns on their respective sheets.
5. Write the headings down on top of each column:

   Column 1—Name

   Column 2—Place

   Column 3—Animal

   Column 4—Thing
6. Under each heading, ask the players to write only one word starting with the letter 'M' like so:

   In column 1, under 'Name', the player must write the name of a person beginning with the letter 'M' such as Molly.

Under the second column 'Place', the player should name a place starting with 'M' such as Mumbai and so on for all the columns.

7. Remind the players that the clock stops ticking in 60 seconds or as soon as the first player finishes writing in all the four columns—whichever is sooner.

Tickle the Thoughts:

1. Do you know more animals with the same letter?
2. Do you know the capital of Maharashtra?

Goals Achieved:

- Building recall speed
- Building handwriting speed
- Cognitive skills
- Fine motor skills

TICK-TACK TIPS

1. Remember to keep the World Atlas handy.
2. Together with the players, search for the geographical location of various places.

Activity 28

Category Game!

Players: 5 to 6

Getting Ready:

You already have the materials required for this activity:

1. A stopwatch
2. Empty the children's cupboard, and you will have an assortment of clothes such as t-shirts, shirts, pants, shorts, socks, etc.

> **Resources Required:**
>
> 1. A stopwatch
> 2. Children's cupboard and an assortment of children's clothes

How to Play:

1. Ask the players to make categories in the room.
2. Use each corner of the room as a category such as Corner 1 for pants, Corner 2 for shorts and so on.
3. Ask the players to fold all the clothes and place them back into the cupboard as per the categories.
4. Encourage the players to allocate specific areas or drawers of the cupboard for different categories.

Tickle the Thoughts:

How else do you think you can categorize the clothes?

Goals Achieved:
- Categorizing
- Problem-solving
- Breaking complex information into smaller organized bits
- Clear thinking

TICK-TACK TIP

Help the child to organize by arranging things into the categories mentioned below:

'LATCH'. L-Location A-Alphabet T-Time C-Category Ch-Hierarchy.

Association

Num-bet Codes!

Players: 4 to 5

Getting Ready:

Make a list of ten words keeping in mind the child's current reading level.

How to Play:

1. Invite one player to read out a list of 10 words to another.
2. Give the children the coded sheet to read from (given below).
3. Ask the children to refer to the coded sheet and write the given words in a coded language.
4. Help them master the activity, encourage them to write short messages and later, write a few paragraphs.
5. Ask them to read the message such as:
   C4NDY I5 IN 7HE B4G
   (CANDY IS IN THE BAG)
   5H3RRY 4ND G3NI3 AR3 FRI3NDS
   (SHERRY AND GENIE ARE FRIENDS)
6. Next, encourage the children to interchange the messages and ask their peers to decode the message and read it aloud

> **Resources Required:**
> 1. A paper and pen
> 2. Coded message
> 3. Printout of the 'Number-Alphabet' Code

Tickling the Thoughts:

1. Can you read?
2. Until which line were you reading with extra effort?
3. Why do you think you were able to read with ease later?

CODE:

A-4, B-B, C-C, D-D, E-3, F-F, G-G, H-H,

I-I, J-J, K-K, L- L, M-M, N-N, O-O, P-P,

Q-Q, R-R, S-5, T-7, U-U, V-V, W-W, X-X,

Y-Y, Z-2

Goals Achieved:

- Interpretation of words as symbols
- Recalling words from memory
- Working out words by using sound-letter relationships
- Spelling rules and conventions
- Knowledge of root words and affixes
- Writing the word and checking to see if it looks right
- Making analogies to known words or parts of words

TICK-TACK TIPS

1. Ask the children to come up with their own special messages to write on greeting cards for various occasions like, Diwali, Christmas and have them post it for family and friends.
2. Remember to inform your friends about the same!

Morse Code I!

Players: 4 to 5

Getting Ready:

1. Keep ice cream sticks, food grains, A4-sized sheets ready.

2. Use a pencil to draw the letters on the sheet.

3. Make letters out of the play dough so that they fit exactly the ones drawn on the sheet.

4. Remember to make the markings on the letters dark enough for the player to remember where to place the grain and the ice cream sticks.

> **Resources Required:**
>
> A play dough, pulses such as kidney beans, ice cream sticks, paper, pen, A4-sized sheets

How to Play:

1. Help the players to roll out the play dough and make letters.

2. Ask them to place the dough on top of the letters drawn on the sheet. (A reference sheet has been provided on the next page.)

3. Ask them to place a grain on every dot and an ice cream stick on every dark line (dash).

Tickle the Thoughts:

1. Ask them if they can see any correlation between the way they have placed the grains and ice cream sticks on the letters

and the Morse code. (A morse code is a method of relaying messages.)

Goals Achieved:

- Visual processing of information
- Interpretation of words as symbols
- Multi-sensory learning
- Cognitive skills

TICK-TACK TIP

Ask children to come up with their own secret language.

Activity 31

Morse Code II!

Players: 4 to 5

Getting Ready:

Have a paper, pen, print of the Letter Morse Code and the Number Morse Code for each player. (Refer to the picture code provided at the end of this activity.)

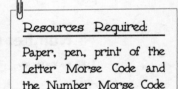

Resources Required:

Paper, pen, print of the Letter Morse Code and the Number Morse Code

How to Play:

1. Explain in a fun manner that every 'dot' is called 'dit' and every hyphen is called 'dah'.
2. Every letter is separated from another letter by three dot spaces.
3. Every word is separated by a line.
4. Invite every player to write a coded message secretly using the Morse Code.

Tickle the Thoughts:

1. Can you read the other player's message? Exchange the sheets!
2. Give the children the coded sheet to read.
3. Next, give them a paper and pen and ask them to write their names, nicknames and names of their pets.
4. Compose a brief message in Morse Code for the children to decode such as: 'The cake is ready.'

Letter Morse Code

A ●—	J ●———	S ●●●
B —●●●	K —●—	T —
C —●—●	L ●—●●	U ●●—
D —●●	M ——	V ●●●—
E ●	N —●	W ●——
F ●●—●	O ———	X —●●—
G ——●	P ●——●	Y —●——
H ●●●●	Q ——●—	Z ——●●
I ●●	R ●—●	

Number Morse Code

1 ●————	6 —●●●●
2 ●●———	7 ——●●●
3 ●●●——	8 ———●●
4 ●●●●—	9 ————●
5 ●●●●●	0 —————

Punctuation

Period	● — ● — ● —
Comma	— — ● ● — —
Colon	— — — ● ● ●
Query	● ● — — ● ●
Apostrophe	● — — — — ●
Hyphen	— ● ● ● ● —
Fraction bar	— ● ● — ●
Parentheses	— ● — — ● —
Quotation marks	● — ● ● — ●

Goals Achieved:
- Multi-sensory learning
- Cognitive analysis of letters
- Visual processing of information

TICK-TACK TIP

Encourage children to learn punctuation and number codes.

Activity 32

Morse Code III!

Players: 2 to 3

Getting Ready:

1. Keep a table bell ready.
2. Copies of the Letter Morse Code and the Number Morse Code. (Refer to the Morse Codes given in the previous activity.)

> **Resources Required:**
> 1. A table bell
> 2. Prints of the Letter Morse Code and the Number Morse Code

How to Play:

1. Explain to every player that every short sound of the bell represents 'dit' and every long sound of the bell represents 'dah'.
2. Ask one player to begin ringing the bell with two to three letter words.

Number Morse Code

1 ●－－－－	6 －●●●●
2 ●●－－－	7 －－●●●
3 ●●●－－	8 －－－●●
4 ●●●●－	9 －－－－●
5 ●●●●●	0 －－－－－

Tickle the Thoughts:

Can you decode the other player's word or message from the sound of the bell?

Goals Achieved:
- Multi-sensory learning
- Audio-Visual processing of information
- Exercises the short term memory

TICK-TACK TIPS

1. Add some humour to the game by asking children to come up with their own coded language.
2. Encourage children to learn Braille and other forms of coded languages.

Challenge the Reader!

Players: 8 to 10

Getting Ready:

Keep paper, 5–6 different-coloured felt pens and a scale ready.

> **Resources Required:**
>
> An A4-sized paper, five to six different coloured felt pens, a scale.

How to Make:

1. Take an A4-sized sheet and cut it into 8–10 chits of equal sizes.
2. Using the coloured felt pens, write the names on each chit. For example, write 'brown' using green colour and 'orange' using a red felt pen.
3. Place these chits in a small bowl.

How to Play:

1. Invite the players to sit in a circle such that all of them can see you.
2. Next, invite the players to pick up a chit from the bowl and read the 'name' of the colour written on it.
3. Reveal the chit to the player only for five seconds.
4. Include variation as per the questions you want to ask the players. For example, write the name of the colour using the same coloured felt pen!

Tickle the Thoughts:

1. Ask the players one by one, what was the name of the colour written on your chit and what was the colour of the felt pen used to write the name of that colour?
2. Which colour's name was written with green coloured felt pen?

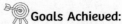

Goals Achieved:
- Enhances concentration
- Visual memory
- Observation

TICK-TACK TIPS

1. Allow the children to gain confidence and then gradually increase the level of complexity.
2. To increase the level of complexity of the game, increase the number of colours to write the names of the colours. You can also make a similar grid (as mentioned in the following activity).
3. Reduce the time given to the child for reading.

Reading Challenge!

Players: 5 to 6

Getting Ready:

Keep an A4-size paper, 5–6 felt pens of different colours and a ruler ready.

How to Make:

1. Using a ruler, draw a grid of five rows and five columns on the paper. In all, you will have 25 boxes or cells.

2. Now, using differently coloured felt pens, colour alternate boxes, leaving a box between two coloured boxes uncoloured. For example, take red, yellow, blue and green felt pen. Then, take a red felt pen and colour the first box. Do not colour the box in the next column. Then, colour the third box yellow and leave out the next or the fourth box blank and so on.

3. Now, using a black felt pen, write the names of the colours in the 'blank' boxes.

4. Add variation to the grid as per the questions you want to ask the players. The grid is ready.

How to Play:

1. Show the grid to the players for 15–20 seconds.

2. Cover the grid.

Tickle the Thoughts:

1. How many colours were there in the picture?
2. Which row or column had the names of all the colours?
3. Was there a box that had the name of the colour written in its own colour?

Goals Achieved:

- Enhanced concentration
- Enhanced picture memory
- Increased observation

TICK-TACK TIP

Allow the children to gain confidence and then increase the level of complexity gradually.

Activity 35

Simon Says!

Players: 8 to 10

Getting Ready:
Set up a play area for 8–10 children.

How to Play:

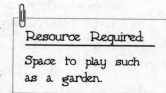

Resource Required:
Space to play such as a garden.

1. One player is named 'Simon' and gives instructions to be executed by the other players.
2. The instructions can be given such as, 'Simon says, touch the colour green', and the children run and touch the green things such as the green colour on a dress, leaves, etc.
3. A player is eliminated if he or she does not follow the instructions properly, or if Simon chases and catches a player who has not touched a green-coloured object yet.
4. The last player is the winner and can give the next instruction as 'Simon.'

Tickle the Thoughts

Ask the children what had the first Simon said.

Goals Achieved:

- Enhanced concentration
- Listening skills
- Following three to four-step commands

TICK-TACK TIP

To further increase the level of complexity, 'Simon' may give a multi-step commands, such as 'Simon says, sit on the floor, jump up high, clap your hands and run to that spot.'

The Pulses!

Players: 2 to 3

Getting Ready:

1. Choose a time of the day when the sun is shining brightly.
2. Ask the child to mix kidney beans and rice on one plate.

How to Play:

1. Ask the child to remove the kidney beans from the mix.
2. Set one minute's time on the stopwatch.

> **Resources Required:**
> 1. 40 to 50 kidney beans
> 2. 250 grams of rice
> 3. 2 plates

Tickle the Thoughts:

1. What are pulses?
2. Name a few pulses.
3. Why is it called kidney bean?

Goals Achieved:
- Enhanced concentration
- Retention of information
- Fine motor skills
- Sensory skills

TICK-TACK TIPS

1. Once the child is able to remove the kidney beans within a given span of time, to increase the level of complexity, increase the number of kidney beans mixed in rice. To further increase the level of complexity, take the black lentil (kali urad dal) and mix it in 50:50 proportion of lentil and rice. Then ask the child to remove the black lentil from the mixture.

2. Another variation could be to mix the black lentil in a play dough.

Find the Word!

Players: 2 to 3

Getting Ready:

1. Keep an identical set of newspaper, magazine or storybook, pens for each player ready.
2. A stopwatch.

Resources Required:

1. A newspaper, magazine or storybook and pens
2. A stopwatch

How to Play:

1. Give each player a sheet of newspaper.
2. Ask them to circle one particular word in the newspaper such as 'they'.
3. Give them two minutes.
4. The player, who finds the most number of 'they' in the newspaper, is the winner.

Tickle the Thoughts:

1. Can you guess how many 'they' are written in the entire newspaper?
2. Which word do you think is the most-used word in a newspaper?

Goals Achieved:

- Enhanced visual memory
- Enhanced 'field of vision'
- Better vocabulary
- Increased pattern recognition
- Enhanced spelling recognition
- Better reading speed

TICK-TACK TIP

If the child finds a spelling of a word difficult to learn, ask him or her to find that word in the newspaper or magazine; the child will soon learn the word visually.

Yummy Sequence!

Players: 2 to 3

Getting Ready:

1. From old recyclable magazines, cut out pictures of different edible items and paste it on an A4-size sheet as shown in the example below.
2. You can also get coloured prints for reference.

> **Resources Required:**
>
> 1. Plenty of recyclable paper or magazines available at home, glue, scissors, A4-sized sheet and prints.
> 2. A stopwatch.

How to Play:

1. Invite a player to look at the picture for 15 seconds and try to remember the sequence of the edibles.
2. After 15 seconds, remove the picture and ask the player to name the edibles in the exact sequence.
3. Once the player has given you the answers, share the picture with him or her and ask the child to self-reflect on the things or sequence he or she might have missed.

Tickle the Thoughts

1. Why do you think you remembered only a few of the pastries?
2. Why did you forget the rest?
3. Now, facilitate the child to make hilarious stories using the

sequence of pictures. (Refer to the example on the next page.)

4. Once the child has made his or her story, repeat the questions again and check the improved recall of the sequence.

Once upon a time, Spiderman wanted to eat a pastry.	But he did not want to eat a pastry with leaves!	Spiderman wanted to eat a strawberry pastry.
So Spiderman spread his web.	But caught a pastry with beads.	And, a pastry with chocolate instead!
So, Spiderman spread his web again.	This time, he caught a strawberry-flavoured doughnut! But he ate it anyway.	After eating eight edibles, Spiderman felt giddy and fell down!

 Goals Achieved:
- Sequencing
- Spatial memory
- Attention
- Association

TICK-TACK TIPS

1. When a significant group of objects that are difficult to remember and spatial arrangements are subjected to change, need to be memorized, this exercise helps to enhance the skills to associate large data to a personal and a funny sequential story.

2. The activity can be repeated by replacing things with actual objects.

3. Allow the child to come up with personal visual associations.

4. Remember to include an element of fun to the story.

5. Remember that there is nothing right or wrong in the story as long as the child is able to associate the visuals in the exact sequence.

Activity 39

Mnemonics!*

Players: 2 to 3

Getting Ready:

Choose a large set of data that might be difficult to memorize.

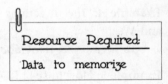

Resource Required:

Data to memorize

How to Play:

1. Ask the child to get a book that he or she finds difficult to memorize, such as a Science or Social Studies textbook.
2. Ask the child to memorize the data in a traditional manner.
3. Now give the child your magical memory clues. Some examples are provided below.

Tickle the Thoughts:

1. Try the following examples with children.
2. Surprise them with the new memory trick called Mnemonics.

Example 1: Names of the planets—Mercury, Venus, Earth, Mars, Jupiter, Saturn, Uranus and Neptune

To memorize, remember: **My V**ery **E**ducated **M**other **J**ust **S**erved **U**s **N**achos

Example 2: Names of the eight US presidents—George Washington,

---

*Remember that Mnemonics help to memorize large information more easily. Mnemonics can be a word, phrase or even a song.

John Adams, Thomas Jefferson, James Madison, James Monroe, John Quincy Adams, Andrew Jackson and Martin Van Buren

To memorize, remember: **Will A Jolly Man Make A Jolly Visitor?**

Example 3: The order of earth's atmosphere—Troposphere, Stratosphere, Mesosphere, Thermosphere and Exosphere

To memorize, remember: **The Silly Monkeys Tickled Elephants.**

Example 4: The directions on a compass—North, East, South and West

To memorize, remember: **Never Eat Sour Watermelons.**

Example 5: How to spell POTASSIUM?

To memorize, remember: One T (tea) and two S (sugar cubes)

Example 6: How to spell NECESSARY?

To memorize, remember: **Not Every Cat Eats Sardines Some Are Really Yucky.**

Example 7: How to spell BELIEVE?

To memorize, remember: Do not be**lie**ve a **lie.**

Example 8: Stalagmites and Stalactites

To memorize, remember: Stala**g**mites are on the **g**round and Stala**c**tites are on the **c**eiling.

Example 9: Vowels—A, E, I, O, U

To memorize, remember: **Aunt Era Ironed Our Uniforms.**

Example 10: What do scientists do? The 'Scientific method' involves, **q**uestioning, **r**esearch, **h**ypothesis, **e**xperiment, **c**onclusion, **r**eport.

To memorize, remember: **Q**uickly **R**un **H**ome **E**ating **C**hewy **R**aisins.

Example 11: Layers of the Earth.

To memorize, remember: Earth has an inner and an outer core, the Mantle and the Crust make four!

Example 12: The waxing or a waning moon.

To memorize, remember: COD

Waxing moon looks like a 'C'. Full moon looks like an 'O', and the waning moon looks like 'D'.

Example 13: The roman numerals—50, 100, 500, 1000.

To memorize, remember: **L**azy **C**ats **D**on't **M**ove.

Example 14: The Metric system prefixes from largest to smallest unit—Kilo, hecto, deka, base, deci, centi, milli.

To memorize, remember: **K**ing **H**enry **D**ied **B**y **D**rinking **C**hocolate **M**ilk.

Example 15: The order of operations for Math—Parentheses, exponents, multiply, divide, add and subtract.

To memorize, remember: **P**lease **E**xcuse **M**y **D**ear **A**unt **S**ally.

Example 16: The speed of light in metres per second is 299,792,458.

To memorize, remember: We guarantee certainty, clearly referring to this light mnemonic.

(The number of letters in each word corresponds to a digit.)

We guarantee certainty, clearly referring to this light mnemonic.

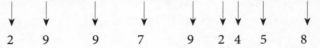

We	guarantee	certainty	clearly	referring	to	this	light	mnemonic
2	9	9	7	9	2	4	5	8

🎯 Goals Achieved:
- Enhances recall
- Associating large data
- Enhanced vocabulary

TICK-TACK TIP

Remember to add the element of fun to the activity for memorizing large data.

Activity 40

Acronyms!

Players: 2 to 3

Getting Ready:

Choose some data to memorize.

How to Play:

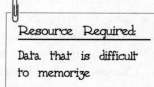

1. Ask the child to get a book that he or she finds difficult to memorize such as a Science or a Social Studies textbook.

2. Ask the child to memorize the data in a traditional manner.

3. Now, give the child memory clues that help him or her memorize large information more easily.

*What are Acronyms?

Some mnemonic devices are also acronyms. A new word formed from the first letters of a series of words and pronounced as a single word is known as an acronym. They are pronounced as a word, for example, NASA (National Aeronautical and Space Administration), and not by spelling out each letter.

Ask the child to tell you the seven coordinating conjunctions or the eight parts of speech of English language. The seven coordinating conjunctions in English—For, and, nor, but, or, yet and so. To memorize this, remember—FANBOYS.

1: The eight parts of speech in English language are—Pronouns,

Adjectives, Verbs, Prepositions, Adverbs, Nouns, Interjections and Conjunctions.

To memorize, remember: PAVPANIC

2: Self-contained Underwater Breathing Apparatus: To memorize, remember: SCUBA

3: Light Amplification by Stimulated Emission of Radiation: To memorize, remember: LASER

4: As Soon As Possible: To memorize, remember: ASAP

5: The United Nations International Children's Emergency Fund: To memorize, remember: UNICEF

6: Day and Time Evolution: To memorize, remember: DATE

7: Ambition in Mind: To memorize, remember: AIM

8: Chariot, Horse, Elephant, Soldier, Sepoys: To memorize, remember: CHESS

9: North East West South: To memorize, remember: NEWS

10: Joy Of Kids Entertainment: To memorize, remember: JOKE

Now, let's have some fun!

11: LOL: Laughing Out Loud

12: ROFLCOPTER: Rolling On (the) Floor Laughing (like a) (heli) COPTER

13: ROFLACGU: Rolling On Floor And Cannot Get Up

Goals Achieved:
- Enhanced recall
- Ability to associate large data for recall
- Enhanced vocabulary

TICK-TACK TIP

Remember to add the element of fun to the activity for memorizing large data.

Abbreviations!

Players: 4 to 5

Getting Ready:

Keep ready large confusing data to memorize such as the matter of a Science or Social Studies textbook.

Resource Required:
Data that is difficult to memorize.

How to Play:

1. Ask the child to memorize the data in a traditional manner.
2. Now give the child memory clues to help him or her to memorize the information more easily.

Tickle the Thoughts:

1. Ask children if they know any abbreviations.
2. Ask them to come up with their own abbreviations.

*What are Abbreviations?

Abbreviations are formed by taking the first letter of a set of words, where each letter is pronounced separately, unlike acronyms. For example:

    B.C. —Before Christ
    A.D —Anno Domini
    A.M.—Ante Meridiem (before noon)
    P.M.—Post Meridiem (afternoon)

E.g.—exempli gratia (for example)
i.e.—id est (that is)
etc.—et cetera (and so on)
Jr.—Junior
Dr—Doctor
NP—No Problem
TTYL—Talk To You Later
TTYS—Talk To You Soon
BRB—Be Right Back
XO—Hugs and Kisses

Goals Achieved:

- Problem solving
- Ability to break large pieces of information into smaller and more manageable bits
- Enhanced recall
- Enhanced vocabulary

TICK-TACK TIP

Remember to add the element of fun to the activity for memorizing large data.

Activity 42

Memorizing Speeches!

Players: 2 to 3

Getting Ready:

Choose an excerpt from a speech to be learnt.

How to Play:

1. Invite the child to read the excerpt once and then role-play delivering the speech, standing in front of all the players—the audience.

2. Suggest some memory clues. For example, for each stanza, help the child to think of 'one' word that explains the key thought.

3. Help the child identify the key thoughts for all the stanzas or pages depending upon the length of the excerpt.

4. Now, ask the child to link all the keywords to create a 'chain of thoughts'.

5. Next, ask him or her to role-play the speech excerpt again, thought by thought!

Resources Required:

1. An excerpt of a speech to be learnt
2. An audience

Tickle the Thoughts:

1. How confident were you during the second time of role-play?

2. When you delivered the speech, did you need to remember all ifs and buts, or did the words simply fall into place by themselves?

Goals Achieved:
- Associating thoughts
- Communication skills

TICK-TACK TIPS

1. Most people fear getting up in front of the people to deliver a speech as they fear that they might forget what they want to actually convey. Encourage the child to remain positive.

2. Choose the keywords that convey the entire thought of the stanza.

3. Allow the child to choose and underline the keywords.

4. Ask the child to link the keywords into a chain of thoughts.

5. Allow the child to deliver the excerpt thought for thought rather than word for word.

6. If the child needs to learn the excerpt word for word, facilitate the child to review them and go over the excerpt often.

Activity 43

Memory Spell!

Players: 2 to 3

Getting Ready:

1. Keep a list of spellings ready that the player usually gets wrong.
2. Paper, pencil or pen for each player.

Resources Required:

1. The list of spellings the child usually gets wrong.
2. A paper, pencil or pen.

How to Play:

1. Invite a player to dictate the words.
2. Ask another player to write those words down on his or her sheet.
3. Allow the child to self-correct the spellings.

Tickle the Thoughts:

1. Ask the child how many words did he or she get right.
2. Now suggest funny memory clues to the child to learn the spellings.

A few examples are as follows:

1. Wednesday: We were WED on a WEDnesday.
2. Business: We take a BUS for BUSiness.
3. Repetition: My PET learned by rePETition.

4. Friends: In the END, you are a friEND.
5. Principle and Principal: PrincipLE is a ruLE and PrinciPAL is a PAL.
6. Frances and Francis: FrancEs is hEr and FrancIs is hIm.
7. Dessert: DeSSert comes after diNNer.
8. Here: Here is wHERE I live.
9. Stationary and Stationery: StationAry is to stand still, and stationEry is where you find an Envelope.
10. Interrupt: To interrupt is to ERR.

Goals Achieved:
- Enhanced spellings
- Association
- Ability to break down complex 'tasks' into simpler ones.

TICK-TACK TIPS

1. Allow children to be creative and come up with interesting ways to remember spellings
2. Bounce more spellings such as: beLIEve, BALLoon, PIEce.

Activity 44

Rehearse—Rote Learn the Text!

Players: 2 to 3

Getting Ready:

Choose a subject matter that needs to be learned by rote.

How to Play:

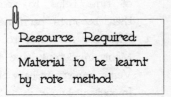

Resource Required:

Material to be learnt by rote method.

1. Give the child the subject matter and set a time limit for him or her to learn it by rote.
2. Note the time taken by the child to learn it.

Tickle the Thoughts:

1. Ask the child to reproduce what he or she has learnt.
2. Note the information the child has missed.
3. Now ask him or her to do it all over again. Only this time, ask the child to establish a visual association with the information to be learned. Then, ask the child to reproduce the information he or she has learned and observe what he or she has been able to reproduce.

Please note that rote learning needs rehearsals and is time-consuming.

🎯 Goals Achieved:

- Association of information with its meaning
- Long-term memory
- Recall large information

TICK-TACK TIPS

1. Rehearsing or recalling the information over a gap of time helps to reinforce the information, which then becomes permanent in the long-term memory.
2. Facilitate the child to segregate information as:
   - Most important–have to know everything about it.
   - Very important–have to know it.
   - Important–know it.

Unscramble the Words!

Players: 2 to 3

Getting Ready:

1. Choose a list of scrambled words.
2. Keep paper, pencil and a stopwatch ready.

> **Resources Required:**
>
> 1. A list of scrambled words
> 2. A paper, pencil and a stopwatch

How to Play:

1. Give the child a list of scrambled words.
2. Depending upon the number of words, set the stopwatch.
3. To begin with, do not set rigid time limits, even though most children enjoy challenging time limits.

Tickle the Thoughts:

1. Which word was the easiest to unscramble?
2. Which word was the most difficult to unscramble?

Goals Achieved:
- Visual memory
- Enhanced spellings and vocabulary
- Enhanced reading speed

TICK-TACK TIPS

1. When you ask the child which was the easiest and most difficult word, you will be able to gauge the level at which the child is. It is from that point that you have to begin and not from the expected level of understanding at school.

2. An 'easier' level of spellings sometimes encourages the child while sometimes he or she loses interest and gets bored. Give your child a well-calculated challenge.

3. While compiling the list of scrambled words, keep the reading level of your child in mind. Refer to the schoolbooks only to understand the level at which the child is expected to be.

4. Get creative with the list; add some humour to your words. Remember, if the child can read a funny six-letter word, the child will be soon competent to read a six-letter word in the school's textbook. You have nothing to lose.

Secret Dictionary!

Players: 2 to 3

Getting Ready:

Keep a dictionary your child is likely to use and papers and pens for each player ready.

How to Play:

Take the child's dictionary and write a secret message on a paper.

How to Write a Secret Message:

Look into the dictionary and replace every word of the message with the preceding word in the dictionary. For example, if your message is, 'Surprise under your pillow', the message to be written could be: 'Surplus undeniable youngster pillory'.

Tickle the Thoughts:

1. Would you like to make a secret message for your partner?
2. What message would you like to convey?

Goals Achieved:

- Enhanced vocabulary
- Word search
- Reading skills

TICK-TACK TIP

Change the format of the secret message. For example, replace the 'preceding' word to the word that follows the actual word in the message such as:

If the message is: 'Surprise under your pillow', the message can be written as, 'Surreal underachieve you're pillowcase'.

Activity 47

Find the Word!

Players: 2 to 3

Getting Ready:

Keep the prints of the given puzzle
and pen or pencil for each player
ready.

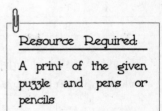

Resource Required:

A print of the given
puzzle and pens or
pencils

How to Play:

1. Give prints of the puzzle and a
   pen each to the players.
2. Ask the players to find and colour or circle the names of
   rivers in the puzzle. One has been done for you.

Tickle the Thoughts:

1. Do you know the names of more rivers?
2. Do you know the place from where the river originates?
3. What do rivers give us?

M	A	H	A	N	A	D	I	X	N
X	K	A	V	E	R	I	E	O	A
T	G	W	T	J	R	Y	N	G	R
G	O	D	A	V	A	R	I	T	M
A	D	M	P	Q	R	B	N	H	A
N	A	P	T	X	B	H	D	J	D
G	V	X	I	Y	A	M	U	N	A
A	A	Q	T	R	J	G	S	W	R
C	R	T	F	Y	X	Z	H	Q	Z
R	I	B	K	R	I	S	H	N	A

Answers:
GODAVARI, INDUS, GANGA, YAMUNA, NARMADA, KRISHNA, KAVERI, MAHANADI, GODAVARI, TAPTI

🎯 Goals Achieved:
- Visual word search
- Information bank
- Enhanced reading skills

TICK-TACK TIP

Design the crosswords keeping the interests of the child in mind. For example, if the child is interested in cycles, design the crossword about the parts of the cycle. The idea is to get the child interested in finding words.

Antonym Crosswords!

Players: 2 to 3

Getting Ready:

Keep a print of the given crossword fixed on a clipboard and a pen or a pencil for each player ready.

*Antonyms represent the opposite of the given word, such as day—night.

How to Play:

1. Share one print with each player.
2. Explain to the player that 1-Across means the antonym has to fit into the horizontal boxes, starting from the one that says 'number 1'.
3. 1-Down means that the player has to fit the antonym vertically in the boxes, starting from the one that says number 1, without erasing the letter already written in the other boxes.
4. Written clues are given for the players to guess the antonym word that fits in.
5. Do not show the answers until every player has finished their crossword.

ACROSS
1. POOR
2. DIM
3. PRETTY
4. LOW

DOWN
1. WRONG
2. SOFT
3. SMOOTH
4. OLD

🎯 Goals Achieved:

- Analytical skills
- Sequencing logical thought processes
- Problem-solving skills

TICK-TACK TIP

You can make more crossword puzzles that are specific for the child such as a math crossword, using an Excel Sheet.

Message for the Aliens!

Players: 2 to 3

Getting Ready:

1. Choose an open space like a beach and things found in a natural habitat, such as sticks or large pieces of driftwood.
2. A short message for aliens.

> **Resources Required:**
> 1. Open space
> 2. Things found in the surroundings like sticks, etc.
> 3. A message for the aliens

How to Play:

1. Ask the children to imagine that a UFO has crossed the blue sky. Would they like to convey a message to the aliens?
2. Brainstorm with the children what message they would like to convey to the aliens.
3. Make them write the message in a large font so that it can be read by an alien travelling in a UFO or even passengers travelling in the airplanes.

Tickle the Thoughts:

1. Do you think they can read your language?
2. Which language do you think they would understand?

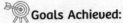
Goals Achieved:

- Enhanced vocabulary and the ability to spell out words
- Teamwork

TICK-TACK TIP

Allow children to come up with funny messages or even funny faces.

Activity 50

Sentence Race!

Players: 20 to 25

Getting Ready:

1. Choose an open safe area or a playground for this activity.
2. Keep lots of flashcards in baskets.

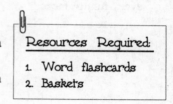

Resources Required:
1. Word flashcards
2. Baskets

How to Play:

1. In the playground, mark the start line and three equidistant areas.
2. Make four teams of children; each group will represent a part of a sentence such as an article, verb, etc.
3. Make the four teams stand at the start line with their flashcards.
4. At the count of three, the first group of children would run towards the second set of children ready to take on the race after getting the first set of flashcards.
5. The second runner will receive the flashcards and quickly choose and pick-up the second flashcard from the basket. The flashcard will form the next word in the sentence.

For example:

1. At the start line, the child will stand holding a flashcard that reads 'I'. The child runs with the flashcard to his or her

teammate standing at the second marking with their set of basket full of flashcards.

2. The two together pick up a flashcard that goes with the first word such as 'am', then the second child runs to the third teammate standing ready with a basket full of flashcards and together, they select a word from the basket that goes with the first two words and so on.

3. They finish the race with a meaningful sentence.

Tickle the Thoughts:

Ask the team to read the new sentence they made together and talk about the new sentence formed.

Goals Achieved:
- Speed reading
- Teamwork
- Gross motor skills

TICK-TACK TIP

Later mix all the flashcards and ask the team to pick out more sentences using them.

Activity 51

Alliteration Genius!

Players: 2 to 3

Getting Ready:

Keep enough time to play together as well as some papers and pencils for each player ready.

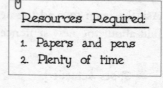

Resources Required:
1. Papers and pens
2. Plenty of time

*Alliteration is the use of same letters or sounds at the beginning of closely connected words in a sentence. For example,

- Guglee Googles and Googles!
- Poor Peter pet the pet.

How to Play:

1. Give each player a number and ask the player number one, to choose any letter such as 'D'.
2. Let children come up with funny alliteration sentences.
3. Give each player his or her turn.

Tickle the Thoughts:

Now, give the players the beginning letters and ask them to make alliteration sentences.

1. Ask them if they can take the first letter of their names and make alliteration sentences that consists of the games they like.

🎯 **Goals Achieved:**
- Phonological awareness required for reading skills
- Auditory memory
- Reading skills

TICK-TACK TIP

You can play this game with children while waiting in the long queue for an appointment or going for a long drive.

Riddles!

Players: 2 to 3

Getting Ready:

Keep a list of riddles ready.

Resource Required:

A list of riddles

How to Play:

1. Keep the answers hidden.
2. Give the list of riddles to one child and ask him or her to read it one by one.

Tickle the Thoughts:

1. Q: What kinds of keys don't open doors?
   A: Donkeys, Turkeys, and Monkeys!
2. Q: What kind of key will open the window?
   A: Keypad
3. Q: What's green and has four wheels and flies?
   A: A Garbage Truck!
4. Q: What time is it when an elephant sits on a fence?
   A: Time to get a new fence.
5. Q: What's green, grows on the ground and has wheels?
   A: Grass. I lied about the wheels!
6. Q: Where do bees go to pee?
   A: The BP Station
7. Q: Why did Tigger look in the toilet?
   A: He was trying to find Pooh.

8. Q: Which two words contain the most letters?
    A: Post office
9. Q: If you have it, you want to share it. If you share it, you don't have it. What is it?
    A: A secret.
10. Q: If you had 5 mangoes and 2 bananas in 1 hand and 2 mangoes and 4 bananas in the other. What would you have?
    A: Very large hands!

Goals Achieved:
- Thinking out of the box!
- Examining the logic of an argument and relating evidence to the conclusion.

TICK-TACK TIPS

1. Riddles are difficult questions that put the child in a dilemma while solving. He or she will need to focus to solve them, as they are not very easy. Keep the fun element alive.

2. Weave riddles in your day-to-day conversations with the child for best results, it makes the child constantly jog his or her memory.

Brain Teasers!

Players: 2 to 3

Getting Ready:

1. Have enough time to play together.

2. Keep ready papers, colour pencils and coloured prints of the given worksheet below.

How to Play:

1. Give a print of the sheet to each child.

2. In the given patterns, the child has to invert the patterns, i.e., in the second column, he or she has to make the outer rectangle grey and the inner triangle black.

3. Some patterns have been provided for reference on the next page. In the first column, parents or facilitators can choose to colour and then handover the sheets to the children.

4. The child can then invert the colour patterns.

Resources Required:

1. Coloured prints of the given worksheet

2. Papers, colour pencils for each player

Column A	Column B

 Goals Achieved:

- Visual memory
- Attention
- Eye for detail
- Enhanced pattern recognition
- Fine Motor Skills

TICK-TACK TIPS

1. Design or draw the worksheets for your child depending on the level of the child.
2. Keep plenty of extra blank space on the worksheet.

Name that Rhyme!

Players: 8 to 10

Getting Ready:

1. Keep some time and undivided attention for your child
2. Please choose a time and place where everything is quiet.

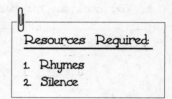

Resources Required:
1. Rhymes
2. Silence

How to Play:

1. Assign each child a number and ask him or her to hum a rhyme or popular song one by one.
2. Remember not to voice out the lyrics of the rhyme.
3. Assign a number to each player and ask the first player to hum the rhyme.
4. Ask all the other players to guess the rhyme.
5. The player who guesses the rhyme first gets to hum the next rhyme.
6. Remember to give each child a chance.

Tickle the Thoughts:

Ask the children to role-play without saying the lyrics of the rhyme and encourage the other players to guess the name of that rhyme.

🎯 Goals Achieved:
- Auditory memory
- Music memory

TICK-TACK TIPS

1. You can hum the rhyme or song and do a few dance steps too.
2. You can play the classic game of 'Dumb Charades'.

Activity 55

Music Memory!

Players: 2 to 3

Getting Ready:

1. Choose some music notes (tones, sequences and pitches) that need to be learnt.

2. Have an instrument the child is learning to play, or a table, plate, spoon, etc., ready.

> **Resources Required:**
>
> 1. Music notes (tones, sequences and pitches) that need to be learnt.
> 2. An instrument the child is learning to play

*How to develop music memory?

Play the music and ask the child to reproduce it. The music could be made by tapping the table and producing the same beat. Change the 'instrument' from tapping the table to using a spoon and a plate to produce the same music.

Tickle the Thoughts:

1. What else in your surrounding can produce sound?
2. How can you establish associations between music to be learnt and relevant information?

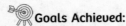

🎯 Goals Achieved:

- Stress management: Pressure before the music exam is minimized
- Listening skills

TICK-TACK TIPS

1. Listen to other musical performance such that you can hear the music in your head.
2. Play the music in slow motion to attain perfection.
3. Rectify the mistakes in memory rather than in the scores.
4. Change the location of practice whenever possible.
5. Change the beginning, such as begin the rhyme or song from the second stanza.

Activity 56

Dino-Attack!

Players: 2 to 3

Getting Ready:

Choose a book to read and keep a dice, print of the game and counters ready.

> **Resource Required:**
>
> Reader, dice, counters, a print of the game

How to Play:

1. Roll the dice, count the dots and move the counter.
2. Use the word in the box to make a sentence to get the next turn. For example, a player rolls the dice and gets five dots. He or she moves the counter to five places where the word 'ask' is written. Then, he or she makes a sentence with the word 'ask' to get the next turn.
3. If the player cannot make a sentence, he or she misses the next turn to roll the dice.
4. The next player helps in making a sentence and gets an extra turn.
5. The counter reaches a 'Dino', the player goes back the trail.

= – 1   = – 2

= – 3   = – 4

	99 sister	98 family	97 children	96 over
FINISH	81 would	82 these	83 put	84 together	85 here
80 question	79 use	78 grow	77 listen	76 there
61 why	62 GO TO 68	63 another	64 brother	65 hear
60 right	59 myself	58 what	57 make	56 their
41 own	42 little	43 GO TO 100	44 again	45 too
40 were	39 walk	38 take	37 then	36 though
21 her	22 how	23 just	24 know	25 let
20 his	19 first	18 had	17 from	16-May
START	2 an	3 any	4 has	5 ask

ink	94 following	93 only	92 does	91 upon
ose	87 beautiful	88 hair	89 began	90 GO TO 85
ough	74 please	73 school	72 where	71 other
ck	67 don't	68 where	69 easy	70 after
ople	54 laugh	53 answer	52 write	51 before
ten	47 every	48 always	49 could	50 when
TO 40	34 the	33 some	32 high	31 knew
ank	27 put	28 live	29 once	30 by
e	14 are	13 friend	12 him	11 by
ng	7 being	8 have	9 fly	10 into

🎯 **Goals Achieved:**

- Associating visuals to read and make out their meanings
- Reading
- Enhanced vocabulary
- Sentence structure

TICK-TACK TIPS

1. The words in the game are the words used frequently for reading.
2. You can make flashcards of the words using a black marker on white paper and place them up on the wall as 'Wall Words'.
3. You can make the environment 'print-friendly' so that the child can refer to the words whenever they have leisure time.

Knowledge

Activity 57

A Long List of Numbers to be Learnt!

Players: 2 to 3

Getting Ready:

Keep a list of numbers to be memorized ready.

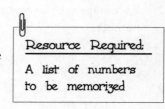

Resource Required:

A list of numbers to be memorized

How to Play:

1. Show a random list of numbers to the child such as 4, 13, 22, 32, 58, 45, 72 and 60, and ask the child to memorize it.
2. Ask him or her to repeat the numbers in the given sequence.
3. Help the child to associate each number with meaningful information. For example:

    4: Knock at the door at number 4.

    13: When my Aunt Sally will visit us on 13th. So that makes Aunt Sally 13.

    22: It is my birthday; 22 becomes my number.

    32: Buckle my shoe at 32.

    58: Make her (Aunt Sally) wait at 58.

    43: Climb a tree.

    72: Lucky you at 72.

Now ask the child to cook up a story with these association of numbers such as: There was a knock at the door (4) and Aunt Sally came to visit us (13). It was my birthday (22) and I had to get ready for the party so I buckled my shoe (32). It took me some time and I had to make Aunt Sally wait (58). While she was waiting for me, she got bored and climbed a mango tree (43). She came down safely and I said to her, 'Lucky you at age 72!'

Tickle the Thoughts:

1. Ask the players if learning the numbers is easier by associating them with meaningful information.
2. Encourage the players to make their own stories for learning numbers.

Goals Achieved:
- Memory recall
- Numeracy
- Creative skills

TICK-TACK TIPS

1. Gradually increase the numbers in the list.
2. Allow the child to establish strong associations so that memory is enhanced.
3. Allow the child to add some humour to the story.

Activity 58

Teach and Learn!

Players: 2 to 3

Getting Ready:

1. Choose a topic that the child will teach the 'students'.
2. Keep notebooks and pen or pencil for each student ready.

Resources Required:

1. A topic to teach
2. Notebooks and pen or pencil for each student

How to Play:

1. Ask the group of children who would like to play a role of a teacher and those who would prefer being students.
2. Give the 'students' notebooks and pens or pencils for taking down notes as they would do in a classroom setting.
3. Give the 'teacher' a topic to teach.
4. Allow the students to ask questions as they would do in the classroom.

Tickle the Thoughts:

1. What would you prefer in a role-play—a teacher or student?
2. Did you find it difficult to answer your students?
3. Do you think, as a teacher, you would require to self-study?

🎯**Goals Achieved:**
- Breaking down complex information into smaller and organized bits.
- Responsibility, self-reflection and self-correcting learning, social skills.
- Motivated to better prepare for future learning.

TICK-TACK TIP

To keep the interest alive, help the child choose a topic he or she is more confident about.

Activity 59

The Name Game I!

Players: 2 to 3

Getting Ready:

Keep a list of names of the player's friends ready.

> **Resource Required:**
> A list of the player's friend's names

How to play:

1. Ask the child to remember the names of people they are not so familiar with. It could be a name of your friend, a plumber or carpenter who has visited your home.
2. Now ask the child to spell the name of a friend in the reverse order such as: KUBER = REBUK

Tickle the Thoughts:

After three to four days, ask the child the friend's name. Expect surprises!

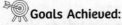**Goals Achieved:**

- Enhanced ability to spell words
- Enhanced memory

TICK-TACK TIP

To begin with, do not give complicated or long names.

The Name Game II!

Players: 2 to 3

Getting Ready:

1. Keep the names of each player's friends ready.
2. A sheet of paper and a pencil fixed on a clipboard for each child.

> **Resources Required:**
>
> 1. A list of the player's friend's names
> 2. Papers and a pencil fixed on a clipboard for each child
> 3. A print of the given code

How to Play:

1. From A to Z, assign a number for every letter, starting from A=1, B=2 and so on.
2. Write the name of the child in numbers and give it to him or her to decode. For example:

4, 9, 22, 25, 1, 13 = DIVYAM

Tickle the Thoughts:

1. Can you guess the numbers of your name?
2. Children love to find the codes for their own names. Hence, allow them to write their own codes.

A=1, B=2, C=3, D=4, E=5, F=6, G=7, H=8, I=9, J=10, K=11, L=12, M=13, N=14, O=15, P=16, Q=17, R=18, S=19,T=20, U=21, V=22, W=23, X=24, Y=25, Z=26

Goals Achieved:

- Numeracy skills
- Decoding information
- Investigation skills
- Inquiry-based learning

TICK-TACK TIP

Ask the children to make codes for the children whom they play with everyday.

Activity 61

Multiplication Tables!

Players: 2 to 3

Getting Ready:

Keep a musical instrument and flashcards of Multiplication Tables ready.

> **Resources Required:**
> 1. Flashcards (provided)
> 2. A stopwatch

How to Play:

1. Ask one player to recite a multiplication table. Begin with the familiar ones such as the table of 2.

2. Now sing the multiplication table with a familiar rhyme such as 'Yankee Doodle Went to the Town': Yankee Doodle Went to the Town 2, 4, 6, 8, 10, 12, 14, 16, 18, 20, 22 and 24, 26, 28 and 30. Similarly, for the table of 9, you can use the rhyme 'Lullaby and Goodnight' and sing the table as: 'Lullaby and Goodnight' 9, 18, 27, 36, 45, 54, and 63, 72 and 81, 90, 99 and a hundred and eight!

3. While the singer is reciting the rhyme, ask another player to show the answers to the singer.

4. Add some music by playing the guitar or by simply tapping on the table.

Tickle the Thoughts:

1. Which is your favourite rhyme?
2. Which table do you think will fit into your favourite rhyme?
3. Allow them the time to experiment singing their favourite rhyme with the multiplication table!

Goals Achieved:

- Pattern recognition
- Incorporating 'math' into 'music'

TICK-TACK TIP

Most children find math a difficult subject. Remember to add music to Math to keep things light.

Activity 62

Master Player!

Players: 4 to 5

Getting Ready:
Keep sports equipment that players enjoy the most, such as football or cricket, ready.

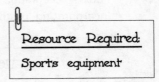

Resource Required:
Sports equipment

How to Play:

1. Invite one child to be the mentor for teaching cricket.
2. Allow all the children to teach a game that they are good at. For example, if the player is a fast bowler, allow him or her to share his or her knowledge and experience about being a bowler.

Tickle the Thoughts:

1. Do you like to bat, bowl or field?
2. Is wicket-keeping a part of fielding?
3. What should the captain do?
4. Where have you seen people play cricket—on TV, roadside, playground, stadium?
5. If given a choice, where would you like to play?

Goals Achieved:

*   Leadership Skills
*   Team work

TICK-TACK TIPS

Explaining a sport or a topic of study:

1. Motivates the mentor to learn, understand and perceive information.
2. Mentoring helps to trigger areas that need more work to enhance memory.
3. Play the game often and assign the responsibilities specific to each child's talent and gradually shuffle the responsibilities.

Pattern Pals!

Players: 20 to 30

Getting Ready:

1. An even number of players.
2. A4-sized paper cards cut into small-sized chits for each player.
3. Pencils or pens for each player
4. A list of the pairs for example:
   - Night and day
   - Bat and ball
   - Hide and seek
   - Bread and butter
   - Cup and saucer
   - Jack and Jill
   - Knife and fork
   - Spaghetti and meatballs
   - Batman and Robin
   - Hansel and Gretel

Resources Required:

1. Even number of players.
2. An A4-sized paper cards cut into four equal halves for each player.
3. Pencils or pens for each player.
4. A list of the pairs.

How to Play:

1. Write down one word of each pair on the pre-cut paper cards.

2. Scuffle and deal one card for each player.
3. Ask all the players to go around the room trying to find their pal (meeting everyone as they go searching for their pal.)
4. The first pair to find their pal is the winner.
5. The game continues till all the pals find their Pattern Pal.

Tickle the Thoughts:

1. Who do you think is your partner?
2. Can you suggest more such Pattern Pals?

Goals Achieved:
- Team work
- Social skills

TICK-TACK TIPS

1. You can incorporate academics. For example, make a list of mountains and their locations or altitudes, trees and their medical names, ice creams and their colours.

2. If you do not have an even number of players, then ask one player to take the lead and give the instructions.

Activity 64

Reflections I!

Players: More the better

Getting Ready:

1. Some water and oil in different vessels, a mirror, blank wall and a brick.
2. A bright room with lots of natural light.

Resources Required:

1. Water and oil in two different vessels, mirror, blank wall, brick.
2. Bright room with all the lights on.

How to Play:

Ask each child to peep into the vessel full of water first and then into the other with oil, then mirror and next, the blank wall.

Tickle the Thoughts:

1. Ask them what is it that they can see?
2. What happened when they looked at the blank wall?
3. How do reflections form? Allow the children time to come up with various answers.
4. Ask them where else they have seen reflections?
5. What is the source of light during the day?

Goals Achieved:

- Inquiry-based thinking
- Leadership
- Team work

TICK-TACK TIPS

1. Encourage the child to write his or her name in mirror script such that the child can read it in the mirror.

2. Ask the child to guess which letters do not change in the mirror.

3. Encourage children to examine objects available in the surroundings and try to find words, which further explain their reflective qualities, such as smooth, polished, varnished, glassy, flat, unruffled, etc. This helps children to develop an eye for (relevant) physical properties of things.

Reflections II!

Players: 2 to 3

Getting Ready:

1. During the day when the sun is shining brightly, have four to five mirrors of different sizes ready in a dimly lit room.

> **Resources Required:**
>
> 1. Four to five mirrors of different sizes and shapes
> 2. Different objects available at home that reflect light
> 3. A dark room

2. Ask the children to take a trip in the house and find as many things as they can that reflects light such as mirrors which change the shape of the reflection, rear view mirrors, spoons, coffeepot lids, buttons, Christmas decorations, copperplates, buckles, bumpers—everything that reflects light.

3. Hang a plane mirror on the ceiling of the dim room.

How to Play:

1. Ask each child to go outdoors and set the angle of the first mirror such that the sunrays fall on the first mirror.

2. Help the child position the first mirror such that the rays from the first mirror reflect and pass through the window of the dimly lit room.

3. Help the child to position the mirror in a way that reflects

the light from the first mirror onto another on the ceiling of the dimly lit room.

4. Allow children to position the objects they had collected from home to reflect light.

5. Now that the light has brightened the dimly lit room, ask the children to place more mirrors in the room to reflect the light from the mirror on the ceiling until the room has adequate lit up.

Tickle the Thoughts:

1. Where else do we use mirrors?
2. What else do you think can reflect light?

Goals Achieved:
- Inquiry-based learning
- Teamwork

TICK-TACK TIPS

1. Encourage children to place a small object like a dice between two mirrors held upright at an angle. Enjoy counting the images with them.

2. Help them change the angle to 180°, 90°, 60°, 45° and 30°.

Chocolate Sandwiches!

Chefs: 2 to 3

Getting Ready:

Keep the following ingredients ready:

> 1 loaf of brown bread
> 1 tin of condensed milk
> 100 gm drinking chocolate
> 10 sweet biscuits
> 1 cup caster sugar
> 2 bowls
> A child-safe knife

Time required: 10 minutes

Resources Required:

1 loaf of brown bread, 1 can of condensed milk, 100 g of drinking chocolate, 10 sweetened biscuits, 1 cup caster sugar, 2 bowls, 1 child-safe knife

Method:

1. Empty the contents in different bowls.
2. Ask the child to cut out the sides of the bread using a child-safe knife.
3. Ask him or her to take one biscuit and dip it in condensed milk for 2 to 3 seconds and place the biscuit on the bread to make it into a sandwich.
4. Let the child place this bread and biscuit sandwich in the drinking chocolate powder.
5. Garnish the chocolate sandwich by sprinkling little caster sugar.

Goals Achieved:
- Following multiple step instruction
- Mathematical skills

TICK-TACK TIP

To garnish the sandwich, one can also use grated coconut powder or even a chocolate sprinkle.

Ice Cream Sundae!

Chefs: 2 to 3

Getting Ready:

Vanilla ice cream, your child's favourite jam, gems or M&Ms, microwave-safe bowl, spoons, glasses (transparent).

Time required: 5 to 7 minutes

> ### Resources Required:
> 1. Vanilla ice cream, your child's favourite jam, gems or M&Ms.
> 2. A microwave-safe bowl, spoons and glasses

Method:

1. Ask the child to take two scoops of vanilla ice cream and put them in a transparent glass.
2. Now ask him or her to take two teaspoons of jam in a small microwave-safe bowl and microwave it for 25 to 30 seconds until the jam turns into liquid syrup. (Adult supervision is required.)
3. Next, ask the child to pour this liquefied jam on the ice cream.
4. Encourage them to garnish the sundae with M&Ms or gems
5. The ice cream sundae is ready to be served.

Goals Achieved:
- Following multiple step instructions
- Mathematical skills

TICK-TACK TIP

To garnish the fruit sundae, the child can also use long wafer biscuits or a layer of cake at the bottom or crushed chocolate biscuits.

Activity 68

Fruit Sundae!

Chefs: 2 to 3

Getting Ready:

Vanilla ice cream, pre-cut fruits of different colours like bananas, pomegranate, mangoes, grapes, strawberries, and spoons, glasses.

Time required: 10 minutes

Resources Required:

1. Vanilla ice cream, pre-cut fruits of different colours like bananas, pomegranates, mangoes, grapes, strawberries.
2. Glasses or goblets and spoons.

Method:

1. Ask the child to take one or two scoops of vanilla ice cream and put them in a transparent glass.
2. Now ask the child to place a fruit of one colour and one layer of ice cream alternately. For example, place a layer of pomegranate and then a layer of ice cream, and again a layer of mangoes followed by a layer of ice cream and so on until the glass is full.
3. The fruit sundae is ready to be served.

Goals Achieved:
- Following multiple step instructions
- Sensory skills

TICK-TACK TIP

To garnish the ice cream sundae, the child can also use wafer biscuits or crushed chocolate biscuits.

Fruit and Veggies Salad!

Chefs: 2 to 3

Getting Ready:

1. Pre-cut fruits like bananas, pomegranates, mangoes, grapes and strawberries.
2. Pre-cut vegetables such as lettuce leaves, onions, tomatoes.
3. Mayonnaise sauce, salt and pepper.
4. Spoons and glasses or goblets.

Time required: Ten minutes.

Resources Required:

1. Fruits like bananas, pomegranates, mangoes, grapes and strawberries.
2. Vegetables such as lettuce leaves, onions, tomatoes
3. Mayonnaise sauce, salt and pepper.
4. Spoons, glasses

Method:

1. Ask the child to mix all the pre-cut fruits and vegetables.
2. Then ask him or her to add 1 tablespoon of mayonnaise sauce to the mixture.
3. Next, add salt and pepper to taste.
4. Refrigerate the fruit and veggies salad and serve it cold in a glass.

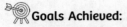

Goals Achieved:
- Following multiple-step instructions
- Mathematical skills

TICK-TACK TIP

Garnish the fruit and veggies salad with rose petals.

Perception

Draw the Best Half!

Players: 2 to 3

Getting Ready:

1. Spend plenty of time to play together.
2. A print of an incomplete worksheet, papers, colour pencils or felt pens ready.

Resources Required:

1. Time to play together
2. A print of the worksheet, paper, colour pencil or felt pens

How to Play:

1. Give the print of an incomplete worksheet to the child.
2. Ask him or her to complete the picture and colour it too.

Tickle the Thoughts:

1. What will you get if you add the remaining half of the picture?
2. Can you guess the name of the transport?
3. Does it fly in the air or travels on road?
4. Which is the fastest means of transport?

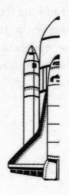

🎯 Goals Achieved:
- Abstract thinking
- Drawing from memory

TICK-TACK TIP

After the child has mastered drawing the second half of the picture using abstract thinking skills, allow him or her to draw their favourite things. For example, if the child likes to draw cars, ask him or her to design a new car with features that he or she thinks should be in the car. Keep talking to the child about the car. The results will surprise you!

Young Picasso!

Artists: 1 to 2

Getting Ready:

1. Spare plenty of time to talk and play together.
2. Papers, colour pencils or felt pens.

Resources Required:

1. Time to play together
2. Paper, colour pencil or felt pens

How to Play:

1. Give each child a sheet of paper and the required stationery.
2. Ask him or her to draw whatever they want.

Tickle the Thoughts:

1. 'This looks really nice!' 'You are an artist!' 'Tell me more about the drawing!'
2. 'This colour looks amazing here! I want to know, have you seen this before?'
3. 'Your imagination is so good that I want you to explain it to me.'
4. Ask the child to draw his or her favourite thing with added features.

Goals Achieved:

- Abstract thinking
- Drawing from memory
- Free thinking
- Fine motor skills

TICK-TACK TIPS

1. Preferably, give the child a huge canvas with lots of space such that the child does not have to restrict his or her imagination due to space constraints.
2. Do not suggest to the child what to draw or how to draw; allow his or her imagination to flourish.
3. Once the child has finished drawing, ask him or her questions with lots of compliments as suggested under 'Tickle the Thought' and the results will surprise you!

Activity 72

Picture the Scene!

Players: 2 to 3

Getting Ready:

A print of the given reference sheet, colour pencils and a clipboard.

How to Play:

┌─────────────────────────────┐
│ Resources Required: │
│ ─────────────────────────   │
│ A print of the sheet,   │
│ colour pencils, clipboard, │
│ for each player   │
└─────────────────────────────┘

1. Give each child a sheet and a pencil or pen.
2. Ask them to draw, write and explain the scenes in five to six sentences.

A few scenes that the child can explain are suggested below:

1. You arrive at the airport and get to know that you have missed the flight!
   Draw the scene.

_____
_____
_____
_____
_____
_____

2. Imagine if your school bag begins to talk. What secrets would it uncover?
   Draw the scene.

_____
_____
_____
_____

3. Imagine if your pillow begins to talk. What are the dreams it would begin to talk about?
   Draw the scene.

_____
_____
_____
_____
_____

🎯 Goals Achieved:
- Thinking skills
- Expressing imaginative visuals

TICK-TACK TIPS

1. You can ask more abstract questions where children must come up with written or oral answers.

2. Do not put restrictions of time, colour, materials used, style of drawing, and orientation of the drawings. Allow the child to think and come up with novel ideas. Listen to your child while he or she is explaining the drawing to you. Share open-ended ideas such that it builds the child's confidence in his imagination. History has been a testimony to the fact that had we not allowed children to think freely, new inventions would never have happened! To invent new things, we need to allow children to think without limitations.

Story-time!

Players: 2 to 3

Getting Ready:

Choose a time of the day when there is not much disturbance in the surroundings.

How to Play:

1. Assign a number to all the players.
2. Introduce a story with a single memorable word.
3. Invite the next player to say that word you had mentioned and create a story with another word.
4. Another player says the first two words and adds a third, and so on.

Tickle the Thoughts:

Ask the players:

1. Who said, (restate the word one of the players had mentioned while fabricating the story)?
2. Invite players one by one to retell the story in their own words.

Goals Achieved:

- Concentration
- Vocabulary building
- Sequence of words, plot building
- Taking turns, team work

TICK-TACK TIPS

1. Alternatively, you can build the story sentence by sentence.
2. Keep the sentences short and simple.

A New Character in the Story!

Players: 2 to 3

Getting Ready:

1. Choose a time of the day when there is not much noise in the surrounding.
2. Keep a storybook ready

```
Resources Required:
1. Undivided attention
2. Time
3. A storybook
```

How to Play:

1. Present a number to all the readers.
2. Read one part of the story aloud to the child.
3. Invite the next reader to read the next part of the story and so on.

Tickle the Thoughts:

1. Ask the child how many characters were there in the story.
2. Invite the child to retell the story in his or her own words.
3. Ask the child to introduce one more fictitious character in the story and describe the newly introduced character.

 Goals Achieved:

- Concentration
- Vocabulary building
- Sequence of words

- Plot building
- Taking turns
- Team work

TICK-TACK TIPS

1. You can build the story sentence by sentence.
2. Keep the sentences short and simple.

Activity 75

Surprise Character!

Players: 2 to 3

Getting Ready:

1. Keep props such as hand puppets of a bear, tree, house, spoon, toothbrush.

2. Choose a time of the day when there is not much noise in the surroundings.

Resources Required:
1. Undivided attention
2. Time
3. Props such as hand puppets of a bear, tree, house, spoon, toothbrush

How to Play:

1. Allocate a number to all the storytellers.
2. Hand a prop to each storyteller.
3. Ask the first storyteller to begin the story with one sentence about the prop.
4. Ask the next storyteller to add a sentence to the sentence given by the first storyteller, using their props and so on.
5. Next, add a new prop that is totally different from the storyline such as a spoon or a toothbrush.

Tickle the Thoughts:

1. At the end of the story session, ask the child to retell the story in their own words.

2. Ask the child: 'Which character said...?'
3. Ask the child: What if the next storyteller had said (introduce a novel situation) instead of...?

Goals Achieved:
- Concentration
- Vocabulary building
- Sequence of words, plot building
- Taking turns, team work
- Creativity

TICK-TACK TIPS

1. Keep the sentences short and simple.
2. In the next story session, interchange the props with the storytellers.

Activity 76

A Bag Full of Stories!

Players: 2 to 3

Getting Ready:

1. Choose a time when there is not much noise in the surrounding.
2. Have seven to eight props ready in the bag.

Resources Required:

1. Undivided attention
2. Time
3. An opaque bag with seven to eight props from the ecosystem like toy trees, mountains, birds, animals, twigs, etc.

How to Play:

1. Allocate a number to all the storytellers.
2. Do not show the storytellers what is inside the bag.
3. Invite them to put their hands inside the bag and guess what is inside it.
4. Then ask the storytellers to pull out one object from the bag and make a sentence about that object.
5. Ask the next storyteller to do the same and build the story using the previous storyteller's sentence and their own props.

Tickle the Thoughts:

At the end of the story session, ask the child to retell the story in their own words.

1. Ask the child: Which character said, '(paraphrase a question from the story)?'
2. Ask the child: What if the next storyteller had said, '(introduce a new situation) instead of...?'
3. Retell the story to them but this time, omit a section of a story and ask the child which section of the story you missed out or 'forgot'.
4. Ask the storytellers what else they thought could have been inside the bag?

🎯 **Goals Achieved:**
- Concentration
- Vocabulary building
- Abstract thinking
- Sequence of ideas, plot building
- Taking turns
- Team work

TICK-TACK TIPS

1. Keep the sentences short and simple.
2. Introduce academic topics like food chain, water cycle through stories.

Object Recall!

Players: 2 to 3

Getting Ready:

1. Keep five objects such as a pen, notepad, pencil, toy, napkin and a few pebbles on a tray.
2. Keep a stopwatch.

Resources Required:

1. Five different common objects such as a pen, a notepad, a pencil, a toy, a napkin, pebbles, a tray
2. A stopwatch

How to Play:

1. Ask the child to observe the objects placed on the tray for a minute.
2. Set the timer for a minute on the stopwatch.
3. After one minute, remove or cover the tray with a napkin.

Tickle the Thoughts:

1. How many objects were there on the tray?
2. What was the colour of the notepad?
3. Name the things kept on the tray with which you can write?

Goals Achieved:
- Visual recall
- Categorizing
- Association

TICK-TACK TIPS

1. Later, as the child masters the game, increase the number of objects on the tray and reduce the time given to the child to study the objects.
2. Do not increase the size of the tray unless required.

Recall the Sequence!

Players: 2 to 3

Getting Ready:

1. Keep a book, shell, biscuit, spoon, glue, napkin, toy, scale, tray, an apple and crayons ready.
2. Set the alarm in the stopwatch.

Resources Required:

1. Eight to nine commonly found objects such as a book, shell, biscuit, spoon, glue, napkin, toy, scale, tray, an apple and crayons.
2. A stopwatch

How to Play:

1. While the child is observing, put 8–9 objects on the tray in a sequence.
2. Start the stopwatch.
3. Ask the child to study the objects for one minute.
4. After one minute, cover the tray.

Tickle the Thoughts:

1. How many objects were there on the tray?
2. Which object was placed after the spoon?
3. What was the last thing in the sequence?
4. Which object is found in the sea? Which is found in a garden?

Goals Achieved:
- Sequencing
- Attention
- Accuracy
- Association

TICK-TACK TIPS

1. As the players learn the tricks, increase the complexity of the game by increasing the number of objects placed in a sequence on the tray, and reduce the time given to the child to observe the objects.
2. Do not increase the size of the tray unless required.

Tring-tring the Telephone Game!

Players: 5 to 6

Getting Ready:

Choose a time of the day or night when there is minimum disturbance in the surroundings.

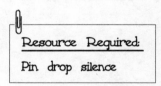

Resource Required:
Pin drop silence

How to Play:

1. Assign a number to each child.
2. Invite the first child to whisper a short message into the second child's ear such that the other players cannot hear.
3. Ask the second player to add another message to that of the first player's and whisper the full message into the third player's ear and so on till the circle is complete.
4. Now ask the last child in the circle to speak out the full message.
5. Go in the reverse order of players to understand where the wrong message got communicated.
6. The player who communicates the wrong message gets eliminated.
7. The last player in the game is the winner.

Goals Achieved:
- Auditory memory
- Sequence of instructions heard

TICK-TACK TIP

Depending upon the age of the children, one can introduce the information on a particular topic. For example, the first child whispers the word, 'butterfly' into the second child's ear and the second child whispers some more information about the colour or the life cycle of the butterfly. More subject related academic information can be incorporated into the game.

Activity 80

Shadow Play Theatre!

Players: More the better

Getting Ready:

Keep an empty carton, wax paper, glue, child-safe scissors, a battery-operated torch or a study lamp and a few hand puppets ready.

Method:

1. Place the carton horizontally along the length of the carton on the floor.

2. Ask the child to cut the opposite sides of the carton lengthwise using child-safe scissors.

3. Remember to not cut the corners of the carton and leave at least 2 inches on each side.

4. Stick wax paper on one side of the cut carton which will be towards the audience.

5. Hand over the puppets to the performer.

6. Switch on the torch and place it behind the child who will deliver the performance.

Resources Required:

1. An empty considerable size rectangular carton such as that of a TV or a refrigerator, wax paper, glue, safety scissors, battery operated torch or a study lamp and a few hand puppets

2. A performer and audience

How to Play:

1. Ask the child to pick up the objects or puppets and place them in-between the light source and the inside of the carton so that the shadows form on the wax paper.
2. Ask the child to show shadows of different objects to the audience.
3. Ask the audience to guess the object.

Tickle the Thoughts:

1. How do shadows form?
2. Enquire what will happen if the torch is switched off?
3. Allow the children time to come up with various answers and then switch off the torch.
4. Ask them if they can make shadows with their hands.
5. Where else do we see shadows?
6. Where does the shadow go at night?
7. What is the source of light during the day?

Goals Achieved:

- Stage performance
- Composing
- Planning
- Producing
- Executing and performing
- Abstract thinking
- Leadership skills
- Creative thinking

TICK-TACK TIP

Introduce terms such as translucent, opaque and transparent through the creation of shadow puppets and by changing the wax paper with white chart paper and later with black paper.

Activity 81

Maze-amaze!

Players: 2 to 3

Getting Ready:

Keep a carton, ice cream sticks, glue and a chart paper or the print of the maze given on the next page ready.

> **Resources Required:**
> 1. A carton
> 2. Ice cream sticks
> 3. A chart paper
> 4. Glue
> 5. Counters or coins of different sizes

Method:

1. Hand over the stationery to the player and facilitate him or her to draw the maze on the chart paper.
2. Ask him or her to stick the chart paper on the cardboard; let the chart paper dry up for five minutes.
3. Ask the child to stick the ice cream sticks on the lines drawn on the chart paper and allow them to dry.

Method:

1. Give the child all the coins and ask him or her to place the coin at the starting point indicated by an arrow (refer to the picture provided on the next page).
2. Ask the child to slide the coin by tilting the carton towards the finish line.
3. Let the child choose the correct size of coin or button that can slide through the ice cream sticks.

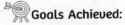

Tickle the Thoughts:

Ask the child which coin do they think will fit in between the ice cream sticks and why? What other materials can they use instead of coins?

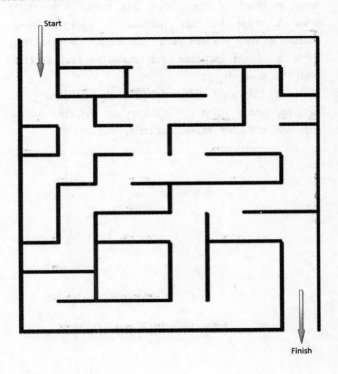

Start

Finish

🎯 **Goals Achieved:**
- Creativity
- Fine motor skills
- Gross motor skills
- Concept of maze
- Problem solving

TICK-TACK TIPS

1. The maze can help in breaking mental barriers for children. If the child tends to 'not see' the objects lying in front of them, then ask them to mentally draw a maze to that particular object in their minds. If they do not find the object where they think it should be, then ask them to find another 'way' to that object.

2. Increase the level of complexity by developing an age-appropriate maze for children on the floor using different coloured tapes, cartons, etc.

Activity 82

Cartographers!

Players: 2 to 3

Getting Ready:
1. Keep a full-sized chart paper and a pen ready.
2. Place a few toys, clothes in a particular corner of a room.

> **Resources Required:**
> 1. A full-sized chart paper
> 2. A pen

Method:
1. Invite a player to draw a simple map of the child's room, living room, or the backyard.
2. Mark out the location of some of the things kept in the room on the map such as a toy or game that you have placed in a particular corner of the room.

How to Play:

Ask another player to find the toys using the map.

Tickle the Thoughts:
1. What do you think these markings (pointing towards the markings you have made) on the chart paper indicate?
2. Who do you think made the first map?
3. What do you think these lines on the map represent?
4. Where are these lines on the earth?
5. If you were to travel by sea route, where will the lines be?

How would you find your way at night if you are travelling by sea?

6. Who was Vasco da Gama?

🎯 **Goals Achieved:**
*   Spatial thinking
*   Representational thinking

TICK-TACK TIPS

1. As the child gets more comfortable using simple maps, encourage them to make their own maps.
2. Take the child outdoors for cycling and encourage them to observe the roads and later make the roadmaps.

I Went to the Park and I...!

Players: 8 to 10

Getting Ready:

Keep some extra time to visit the nearby park.

How to Play:

Resources Required:
1. A visit to the garden
2. A rug

1. Once you are back home from the park, ask the children to sit on a rug and begin the game by saying, 'I went to the park and I climbed a tree.'
2. The neighbouring player says, 'I went to the park and played in the sand, and I climbed a tree.'
3. The next player says, 'I went to the park and played on the swing. I played in the sand and I climbed a tree.'
4. The game continues in a circle with everyone trying to remember all the activities they did.
5. The player who forgets the chain of activities is eliminated.

Tickle the Thoughts:

When the game is over, ask the players who said what.

Goals Achieved:
- Concentration
- Listening skills
- Sequencing

TICK-TACK TIP

To further increase the level of complexity, increase the length of sentence.

I Can Go, With My Eyes Closed!

Players: 2 to 3

Getting Ready:

Draw the maze on an A4-sized sheet and have an eye mask ready to blindfold the players.

> Resources Required:
> 1. Picture of a maze
> 2. An eye mask

How to Play:

1. Place the maze in front of the players on the table.
2. Invite a player and blindfold him or her. Then, ask the player to place their dominant hand's finger on one of the dogs in the maze.
3. Invite another player to direct the first player's finger to the bone that is farthest.
4. As the player moves the finger over the maze, ensure that the moving finger's tip remains in contact with the paper.
5. Once the player has reached the bone, which was the farthest from the chosen dog, ask him or her to move the finger on the page in a straight line and spot the starting point of the game where the dog was!

Tickle the Thoughts:

1. Do you think it is possible to get back to the starting point with your eyes closed?

2. Do you think you can get to your cupboard, pull out a dress and get back to this place without breaking a toe?

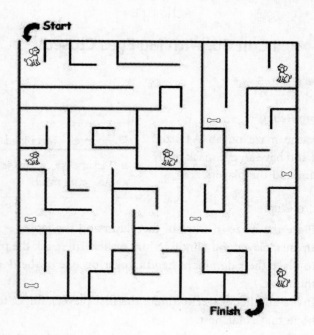

🎯 **Goals Achieved:**
- Enhanced topographical memory
- Enhanced vestibular memory-memory of movement and not of position
- Enhanced recognition of a familiar route or place

TICK-TACK TIP

Ask the child to close his or her eyes and find the way to the kitchen and get a glass of water for you.

Find the Mistake!

Players: 2 to 3

Getting Ready:

Keep some prints of the flashcards provided, child-safe scissors and a stopwatch ready.

Resources Required:

1. Prints of the flashcards (provided below) and child-safe scissors
2. A stopwatch

How to Play:

1. Ask one player to show the flashcards to the other player.
2. Set the stopwatch for 15 seconds.
3. Within 15 seconds, the child has to find the mistake.

Tickle the Thoughts:

1. Was the time given to you challenging?
2. What were you thinking during the 15 seconds?

Flash Card-1

```
oooooooooooooooooooooooooooooooooooooooooooooooooooo
oooooooooooooooooooooooooooooooooooooooooooooooooooo
ooooocooooooooooooooooooooooooooooooooooooooooooooooo
oooooooooooooooooooooooooooooooooooooooooooooooooooo
oooooooooooooooooooooooooooooooooooooooooooooooooooo
oooooooooooooooooooooooooooooooooooooooooooooooooooo
```

Flash Card-2

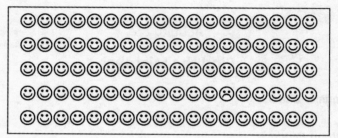

Flash Card-3

AAAA BBBB CCCC DDDD EEEE FFFF GGGG HHHH

IIII JJJJ KKKK LLLL MMMM NNNN OOOO

PPPP QQQQ RRRR SSSS TTTT UUUU VVVW

WWWW XXXX YYYY ZZZZ

Flash Card-4

AAAA BBBB CCCC DDDD EEEE FFFF GGGG HHHH

IIII JJJJ KKK LLLL MMMM NNNN OOOO

PPPP QQQQ RRRR SSSS TTTT UUUU VVVV

WWWW XXXX YYYY ZZZZ

Flash Card-5

YOUYOUYOUYOUYOUYOUYOUYOUYOUYOUYOUYOUYOUYOUYOUY
OUYOUYOUYOUYOUYOUYOUYOUYOUYOUYOUYOUYOUYOOOUYO
UYOUYOUYOUYOUYOUYOUYOUYOUYOUYOUYOUYOUYOUYOU

Flash Card-6

> ## Be kind to the
>
> ## the people who help you.

🎯 **Goals Achieved:**
- Visual memory
- Reading speed!

TICK-TACK TIPS

1. Experiment and exercise with the various types of mistakes provided in the flashcards.
2. Begin by identifying the mistakes in shapes such as in the first flashcard (full circles and semi-circle) and graduate it to letters, then to words, next identify mistakes in sentences.
3. As the player gets trained to recognize mistakes, to increase the complexity, reduce the time each player gets to find the mistake in the flashcard. Also, reduce the font size.

Creativity

Activity 86

Shake the Shakers!

Players: 2 to 3

Getting Ready:

1. Keep a stopwatch and an eye mask ready.
2. Keep various pulses and 6 recyclable bottles that look alike.

Resources Required:

1. A stopwatch and an eye mask
2. Six empty recyclable bottles that are alike.
3. Different pulses that can be put inside the bottle

How to Play:

1. Introduce the different kinds of pulses to the players.
2. Give each player an empty recyclable bottle and ask them to put one type of pulse in one bottle.
3. Then, ask the players to close the lids of their shakers or bottles.
4. Next, using the eye mask, blindfold the first player, and ask another player to hand over a shaker of his or her choice to the blindfolded player.
5. Now, ask the blindfolded player to shake the shaker or bottle and guess the pulses by listening to the sound it makes.

Tickle the Thoughts:

1. Ask the child to listen carefully. Name the pulse is in the shaker.

2. While the child is still blindfolded, offer the child the pulses to feel and match the pulses to the shaker.

3. Ask the child to tell you the name of the pulse.

🎯 **Goals Achieved:**
- Auditory memory
- Sensory skill

TICK-TACK TIP

Different pulses make different noises when the player shakes the shakers. Include variation by replacing the pulses with pebbles and beads.

Activity 87

Paper Planes!

Players: 2 to 3

Getting Ready:

1. Recyclable wedding cards, newspapers or chart papers.
2. Verandah or window.

How to Make Planes:

1. Fold a rectangular paper lengthwise in half.
2. Fold the top two corners of the paper by bringing them to the centre to meet each other. The paper resembles an arrow now.
3. Turn the paper over so that the side facing you, now faces down.
4. Fold the corners again by bringing them to the centre to meet each other.
5. Now, fold the whole paper lengthwise at the centre. Ask the children to go to an elevated area such as a window on the first floor (parental supervision required) and set the plane to fly.
6. The player whose plane travels the maximum distance is the winner.

Tickle the Thoughts

1. How can an airplane made of paper fly but we cannot?
2. What is aerodynamics?

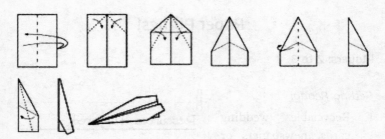

Goals Achieved:

- Following multiple-step commands
- Concentration
- Fine motor skills

TICK-TACK TIP

A paper clip attached to the nose will make the airplane fly even faster.

Bull's Eye Balloon!

Players: 7 to 8

Getting Ready:

Keep balloons ready and draw a start and finish line on the ground using chalk.

```
Resources Required:
1. Balloons
2. Few chalks
```

How to Play:

1. Lineup the players at the start line and assign a number to each player.
2. Give one deflated balloon to each player.
3. Tell the players to blow or inflate the balloon and hold it tight in their fingers.
4. Ask the players not to tie a knot to the balloon.
5. Ask them to let go of the balloon on the count of three.
6. Aiming at the finish line, the player's balloon that falls closest to it is the winner.

Tickle the Thoughts:

1. Encourage the players to think why the balloon gets inflated when they blow air into it?
2. Where did the air come from into the player's mouth?
3. What do they think will happen to the balloons if they let go of them?

4. Will the balloons go up in the air or will they fall on the ground?

Goals Achieved:
- Oro-motor skill development
- Fine motor skills
- Thinking skills
- Concept-building

TICK-TACK TIPS

1. Share information about air and the atmosphere around the earth.
2. Introduce the concept of gravity to the children.
3. Older players can be introduced to the organs such as lungs (an organ where the air is stored to be blown into the balloon) and other body parts as well.

The Amazing Neighbourhood!

Players: 2 to 3

Getting Ready:

1. Take out some extra time to visit your neighbourhood.
2. Intimate the friend whose home you will be visiting.
3. You will also need cardboard, coloured felt pens, pencils, crayons, recyclable containers, dice and notebooks.

> **Resources Required:**
> 1. A visit to a friend's home
> 2. A cardboard, coloured felt pens, pencils, crayons, recyclable containers, dice, notebook

How to Play:

1. Walk to a friend's home.
2. Urge the children to carry their notebooks and pencils with them.
3. Encourage them to read the street signs, intersections, parks, corner stores and other common features of the neighbourhood.
4. Ask the children to make a note of all the things they notice in their notebooks.
5. Mark out the route in squares such as two squares for crossing the street traffic signal.
6. Once all of you are back home, help the children to draw the route by adding more details.

7.   Now roll the dice, move the counters and the player who reaches the destination first, is the winner.

Tickle the Thoughts:

1.   What all things did they see on the way to their friend's home?
2.   Where does your friend live?

Goals Achieved:

- Spatial thinking
- Observation
- Research on how the world works

TICK-TACK TIPS

1.   Introduce the post office and address to the child.
2.   Encourage the child to write a letter to his friend, and after a few days, go to that friend's home to ensure that the letter sent by your child has reached him or her.
3.   Remember to quietly inform the friend to keep the letter safe.

Treasure Maps!

Players: 2 to 3

Getting Ready:

Keep the treasure, pencils, felt pens, paper, two-feet ribbon of any colour and child-safe scissors ready.

How to Play:

1. Ask one player to go to the garden and find a suitable place to hide the treasure.

Resources Required:

1. Pencils, felt pens, paper, 2 feet ribbon of any colour, child-safe scissors
2. A treasure such as a small bag of lollypops.

2. Ask the child to cut the paper into small chits.

3. Help the child to write 6–8 clues on those small paper chits to find the treasure.

4. Write clues such as 'Find the next clue at five steps from the flower bed. Turn right.'

5. Ask the child to hide those chits according to the clues written on them.

6. Ask the other players to look for the clues and find the treasure.

7. The child who finds the treasure is the winner and gets to hide the treasure next!

Tickle the Thoughts:

1. What do you treasure the most?
2. What else do you think can be used as treasures?
3. What makes you think that the place where you want to hide the treasure is going to be difficult for the players to find?
4. How else do you think you can give clues to the players to get to the treasure?

🎯 Goals Achieved:
- Spatial thinking
- Research on how the world works

TICK-TACK TIPS

1. For the children who are more familiar with the game, make the clues really cryptic.

2. For younger children, give clear instructions written in short sentences.

3. Encourage the players to write the clues in Morse code. Use the Morse codes given in the previous activities!

Activity 91

Traffic Signs Game!

Players: 2 to 3

Getting Ready:

1. Have a clipboard for each player, paper or pencil ready.
2. Time to go on a road trip.
3. Set the timer on the stopwatch.

Resources Required:

1. A clipboard for each player, paper, pencil
2. A road trip
3. A stopwatch

How to Play:

1. Give each player a clipboard, a pencil and a paper.
2. While the car is moving, ask the players to spot as many road traffic signs as they can.
3. Ask the players to draw and write as many details about the traffic signs as he or she can remember.
4. One sign can only be spotted once in a game.
5. Set the stopwatch for 30 minutes.
6. After 30 minutes are over, count to see which player has spotted the most signs.

Tickle the Thoughts:

1. How do these traffic lights change colours?
2. What is the purpose of these signs? Alternatively, why do you think these signs have been put up?
3. Who do you think has put up these signs?

4. What else do you think can be put up for the safety of the people?
5. Is it important for us to read these signs, how does it help us?

🎯 **Goals Achieved:**
- Visual memory
- Quick thinking

TICK-TACK TIP

As the car is moving, it gives the child extremely short time to see and observe the signs. Ask the child to remember and recall them from the memory to draw and write about it. To reduce the complexity, slow down the speed of the car. It will provide more time to the child to see and observe.

Activity 92

Eyes on My Head!

Players: 2 to 3

Getting Ready:

Pretend that you are trying to recollect where you have seen 'this' person before!

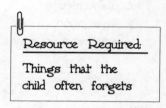

Resource Required:

Things that the child often forgets

How to Play:

1. You enact that you are struggling to remember where you have seen 'this' person such as a juice store owner at the corner of the street.
2. After a minute long struggle, you remember that he is the owner of the juice stall at the end of the street!
3. Allow the children to laugh at your memory skills!
4. Ask them how they think will make remembering people easier.
5. Should you imagine the juice seller with a basket full of apples hanging from his ears or a small leaf from the bunch of grapes tickling his nose and making him sneeze ten times?
6. Ask them how else they can learn names and faces of people whom we see and meet often.
7. Wait for the surprise; allow them to come up with answers!

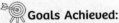

Tickle the Thoughts:

Do you remember Aunt Sally? She was a good cook! Help children to imagine 'Aunt Sally' cooking and serving them their favourite dish.

Do you recognize the librarian? His hair and the colour of the book's pages were the same.

Goals Achieved:

- Association
- Building more connections for long-term memory

TICK-TACK TIP

Help children recall difficult things by including an element of fun to associate with the mundane memories that are easily forgotten. Make learning and remembering enjoyable and interesting.

Activity 93

Dot-to-Dot!

Players: 8 to 10

Getting Ready:

1. Mark an A4-sized sheet with equidistant dots.
2. Pencils for each player.

How to Play:

1. Give pencils to all the players and ask them to sit around the sheet as it is a group game.
2. Assign each player a number.
3. Ask the first player to draw a line connecting two dots.
4. All the players can join any two dots on the sheet but cannot overwrite on the existing line.
5. As players take their turns, the one who gets to complete a rectangle gets to write the initial letter of their name inside the box.
6. The player who makes the rectangle gets a bonus turn to draw another connecting line.
7. When all the dots have been connected, the players count the rectangles with the initial letter of their name. The player with most boxes is the winner.

> **Resources Required:**
>
> 1. An A4-sized sheet with equidistant dots (refer to the image given)
> 2. Pencils for each player

Tickle the Thoughts:

1. What is a 'design'?
2. Can you develop designs using dots?

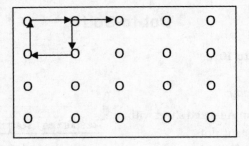

Goals Achieved:
- Eye-hand coordination
- Concentration
- Strategy building

TICK-TACK TIP

Ask the child to find designs present in the natural environment!

Designer's Dots!

Players: 2 to 3

Getting Ready:

1. Organic Rangoli colours.
2. Children with their aprons.
3. An open space, preferably a flat ground.
4. A few flat-bottom sieves.

> ### Resources Required:
>
> 1. Organic Rangoli colours
> 2. An apron
> 3. An open space
> 4. A few flat-bottom sieves as shown in the picture

How to make a rangoli:

1. Ask the children to take a sieve each and place it where they plan to make the design.
2. Ask him or her to pour one of the colours (preferably white) into the sieve and gently spread the powder so that it passes through the holes onto the ground to make equidistant dots.
3. Remember to help the children to pick up the utensil very gently so that the design does not smudge.

4. Now ask the children to choose another colour.
5. Ask him or her to take a pinch of powder, holding it between the thumb and the index finger.
6. Using the colour, ask the child to join the white dots such that a pattern is formed.

Tickle the Thoughts:

1. How else do you think you can make the dots?
2. Which other utensil do you think can be used for making designs?

Goals Achieved:

- Concentration
- Visual skill

TICK-TACK TIP

Help the child to make designs on paper first and subsequently make rangoli or even henna designs.

Tongue Twisters!

Players: 2 to 3

Getting Ready:

Some extra time to spend with the children.

How to Play:

1. This game can be played anywhere. For example, during a long drive or while waiting for an appointment or before sleeping.
2. Keep a sheet of tongue twisters handy, or you can get creative and make some with the children.

Resources Required:
1. Your time
2. Good light mood

Tickle the Thoughts:

1. Invite the children to come up with their own tongue twisters.
2. Ask them if they know of more tongue twisters in their mother tongue.

Some classic tongue twisters are:

1. I scream, you scream, we all scream ice cream!
2. I saw a kitten eating chicken in the kitchen.
3. Four fine fresh fish for you.
4. Red brick, blue brick.
5. Red lorry, yellow lorry.
6. Thin sticks, thick sticks.

7. Good blood, bad blood.
8. A peck of pickled peppers Peter Piper picked.
    If Peter Piper picked a peck of pickled peppers
    Where's the peck of pickled peppers Peter Piper pickled?
9. Betty Botter brought a bit of butter
    But she said her bit of butter's bitter,
    So she bought some better butter to make her bit of bitter
    butter better!
10. How much wood would a woodchuck chuck if a woodchuck
    could chuck wood? He would chuck, he would, as much as
    he could, and chuck as much wood.

Some more popular tongue twisters in Hindi:

1. *Kaccha papad, puckka papad.*
2. *Dubay Dubai may doob gaya.*
3. *Pakay ped par paka papita, paka ped ya paka papita, pakay
    ped ko pukaray Pinku, Pinku pakaray paka papita.*
4. *Kala kabutar safed tarbuj, kala tarbuj safed kabutar.*
5. *Lala Gope Gopal Gapanggam Das.*
6. *Neele rail lal rail, neele rail lal rail.*
7. *Chandni raat may chaar chudhail nay chanay chabay.*
8. *Chandu ke Chacha ne, Chandu ki Chachi ko, Chandani Chauk
    mein, Chandani raat mein, Chandi ke Chammach se chatni
    chatayi.*
9. *Tola Raam tala todkar tel mein tul gaya, tula hua Tola tale
    hue tel mein tal gaya.*
10. *Khadak Singh kay khadaknay say khadakteen hain khidkeeyan,
    khidkeeyon kay khadaknay say khadakta hai Khadak Singh.*

🎯 Goals Achieved:
- Auditory sequencing
- Communication skills

TICK-TACK TIP

All the languages have popular tongue twisters, s̶
funny and some with morals; encourage the chi̶
learn as many tongue twisters as possible.

Pl̶

Get̶

Keep̶
clipb̶

How̶

1. G̶
   a ̶

2. As̶
   slee̶
   the ̶
   cont̶
   2, br̶

3. Conti̶
   again.

4. Then t̶
   down t̶
   again (S̶
   is traced̶

5. Rememb̶
   Do not r̶

the Tho̶

̶e ch̶

Activity 96

Drawing the Infinity!

ayers: 2 to 3

ting Ready:

some papers, colour pencils,
oards ready.

to Play:

ve each child a paper fixed on
lipboard and colour pencils.

the children to begin drawing the infinity sign or the
ping eight starting at the centre of the sheet. Begin with
left loop—draw or trace a line to the top left (Step 1),
inue with a curved line along the left-hand side (Step
ng it down.

nue to the bottom (Step 3), and up through the centre

race the right side-up and over the top right (Step 4),
he right side (Step 5), along with the bottom and up
tep 6) through the centre. The right side of infinity
clockwise.

er to follow the instructions as mentioned.
everse the process of forming the infinity.

ughts:

ildren where else they can form the sleeping eight.

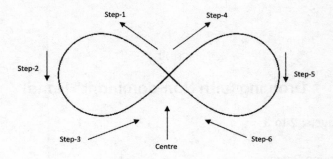

🎯 Goals Achieved:

- Activates and integrates the left and right brain hemispheres
- Enhances vision
- Improves eye-hand coordination

TICK-TACK TIPS

Remember the instructions mentioned above and encourage children to:

1. Draw a sleeping eight (with the centre marked for reference) on the floor using chalk and invite the child to walk on it, closing the sleeping eight back at the centre.

2. Close the fist with the thumb up and out, and move it starting from the centre while the eyes are focused at the tip of the thumb nail.

3. Play a sport like football or badminton with non-dominant leg or hand.

Drawing with Non-dominant* Hand!

Players: 2 to 3

Getting Ready:

Keep a clipboard, paper and pencil for each player ready.

Resource Required:

A clipboard for each player, paper, pencil

How to Play:

1. Give each child a paper fixed on a clipboard and colour pencils.
2. Ask the children to draw as many objects they want using their non-dominant hand.

*If the child uses his or her right hand to do most of the activities, then ask him or her use his left hand to draw. The hand not used frequently is the non-dominant hand.

Tickle the Thoughts:

1. Ask the children if it was as easy as drawing with their dominant hand.
2. How would they manage if they had ten hands?
3. Do you know of artists who make nice paintings without using their hands?

🎯 Goals Achieved:

- Strengthens neural connections in the brain
- Enhances new connections
- Creativity
- Cognitive skills

TICK-TACK TIPS

1. Other activities you can encourage children to use their non-dominant hand:

   Brushing their teeth, bathing, opening jars (using the dominant hand to hold the jar and opening the jar with the non-dominant hand), pouring juice into a bottle with a narrow neck, buttering the toast, playing instruments that require using both the hands, using a computer mouse, using clothes pegs, playing soccer with the non-dominant leg, etc.

Workout for Mid-brain Activation!

Players: 2 to 3

Getting Ready:

1. Spare some extra time to do the workout before the child begins to study.
2. Light and happy workout environment.

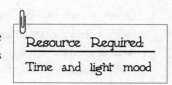

Resource Required:
Time and light mood

How to Play:

1. The exercises mentioned may even confuse adults. Therefore, I suggest that parents try it first.
2. Allow the child to laugh at you sometimes!

Exercise-1

How to perform the exercise:

1. Fold hands in the shape of a 'Namaste'—palm to palm and fingertips to fingertips. Then, distance your palms from each other and the wrists as well, but keep the fingertips joint comfortably.

2. Keeping the fingertips joint, distance the thumbs, and move the thumbs clockwise.

3. After doing 10 rotations, change the movement to anti-clockwise.
4. Then, join the thumbs and start the same rotations with the index fingers, 10 clockwise and 10 anti-clockwise rotations.
5. Continue till the rotations for all the fingers are complete.

EXERCISE-2

How to perform the exercise:

1. Ask the child to show the 'victory sign' with the index and the tallest finger of the right hand and with the left hand ask the child to make the victory sign with its tallest and the ring finger.
2. Next, ask the child to repeat by switching the victory sign to the opposite hands.
3. Repeat the exercise 10 times for each hand simultaneously.

EXERCISE-3

How to perform the exercise:

1. Ask the child to show the 'victory sign' with the index and tall fingers of right hand and a 'wow sign' (join the tip of the thumb and the index finger's tip, while the other fingers are spread open) with the left hand.
2. Now ask the child to make the 'victory sign' with the left hand and the 'wow sign' on the other hand.
3. Switch the exercises to both the hands.
4. Repeat the exercise 10 times for each hand simultaneously.

EXERCISE-4

How to perform the exercise:

1. Ask the child to open his or her index and tall fingers

representing two thieves with the right hand.

2. Ask the child to shoot the two 'finger-thieves' with a 'finger-gun' made with thumb and the index fingers of the left hand.

3. Now ask the child to switch the hands; make thieves with the left hand and gun with the right hands. Switch the hands after every three to five seconds.

4. 10 repetitions for each hand.

Exercise-5

How to perform the exercise:

1. With the elbow stretched outwards, place your left hand almost touching the head, stretch the hand upwards such as the child measures his/her own height, allow the child to repeat this step ten times.

2. Next, ask the child to place the right hand on the belly button, but not touching the belly. Ask the child to move the hand in a circular motion as if the child is saying, 'My stomach is full.' Repeat the exercise ten times.

3. Now ask the child to do both the steps simultaneously with both the hands.

4. Ask the child to repeat the exercise by switching the exercises to the opposite hands.

Exercise-6

How to perform the exercise:

1. Ask the child to close both the hands into a fist.

2. Now ask the child to open the thumb of the right hand and point it in the right direction and simultaneously open the little finger of the left hand and point it in the right direction for 3–4 seconds and then close the thumb and the little fingers.

3. Then, ask the child to switch to the opposite hand, i.e., open the thumb of the left hand and then the little finger of the right hand.
4. Ten repetitions for each hand.

Exercise-7

How to perform the exercise:

1. Ask the child to show you the victory sign with the left hand once again, and with the right hand, ask the child to open the index and the little finger (with the thumb, tallest and ring finger curled in).
2. After 3–5 seconds, ask the child to switch the exercise to the opposite hand and this time open the index and the little finger of the left hand and make the victory sigh with the two fingers using the right hand.
3. Now ask the child to repeat the exercise ten times.

Exercise-8

How to perform the exercise:

1. Ask the child to stand straight and his or her right hand open and right arm stretched in front. Then, tell him or her to make big circles in the space ten times in a clockwise direction.
2. With the left arm stretched in front, ask the child to move it left to right, parallel to the earth without letting the arms to collide.
3. Now ask the child to do both the steps—one and two simultaneously. Repeat it ten times and then switch hands.

Exercise-9

How to perform the exercise:

1. Ask the child to stand straight on the floor and hold the right ear with the left hand and left ear with the right hand.
2. While the child is still holding his or her ears, ask the child to do 10 sit-ups.

Exercise 10

How to perform the exercise:

1. Tell the child to stand straight on the floor.
2. Ask him or her to lift the right knee and gently box the knee with the left hand's fist and vice versa.
3. Rehearse it ten times.

 Goals Achieved:
- Concentration
- Multi-tasking
- Creativity

TICK-TACK TIP

Blindfold the child and ask the child to do various tasks during the day such as taking a bath.

Activity 99

Memory Blind Spots[*]!

Players: 4 to 5

Getting Ready:

Have a list of ten words ready.

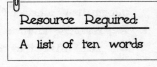

Resource Required:

A list of ten words

How to Play:

1. Invite a child to read out a list of 10 words to other players. For example, pencil, clay, pigeon, tea, glass, storybook, square, balloon, shoe, oil, etc.
2. Now, ask the children to tell you the words in a serial order.
3. Now change the order of words and hear the response of the child, only this time, hear the child recall the words at the beginning and at the end of the serial order.

Tickle the Thoughts:

1. Can you make a word list and help me check my memory too?
2. Allow the child to read out the words to you.

---

*Memory blind spot is the information at the middle of a study session that children miss out. In this activity, when the children are asked to recall the words from a word-list, check the words in the middle of the list such as glass, storybook, square which children might miss out. Increase the number of words in the list to complicate the game.

Goals Achieved:

- Observation and listening skills
- Eye for detail

TICK-TACK TIPS

1. Shuffling the information helps to prevent the creation of memory blind spots.
2. Help the child to focus on the middle part of the information consciously.
3. Repositioning and restructuring of difficult information will help make the child remember the information.

Activity 100

Creating 'False' Memory!

Players: 2 to 3

Getting Ready:

Keep a list of words, paper, pencils, clipboards for each child ready.

Resources Required:

1. A list of 15 words
2. A paper, pencils, clipboard for each child

How to Play:

1. You ask the children to carefully listen to the list of words you are about to say.

2. Ask them to try and remember as many words as they can.

3. Now, read out the following words: Lolly, honey, bitter, bite, sugar, hate, tongue, pastry, cookie, pie, tart, eat, stomach, taste, love.

4. Give each child a paper fixed on a clipboard and a pencil, and ask them to write as many words as they can remember.

5. Next, propose to the children to write 'yes', 'no' or 'not sure' for every four words you are going to give them.

Tickle the Thoughts:

1. Give the children four words in the following order:

2. The first word is 'tongue'. Did the word 'tongue' appear on my word list? Write your answer as 'yes', 'no' or 'not sure.' The second word is a 'wall.' Did the word 'wall' appear on my word list? Ask the children to select and write their answers

as 'yes', 'no' or 'not sure.'

3. The third word is 'tall' in my word list. Did the word 'tall' appear on my list? Write your answer as 'yes', 'no' or 'not sure.'

4. The fourth word is 'sweet.' Did the word 'sweet' appear on my word list? Write your answer as 'yes', 'no' or 'not sure.'

Without much ado, tell them that the memory test is over. Ask them what they wrote for 'sweet.'

Goals Achieved:

- Listening skills
- Dogging the memory

TICK-TACK TIP

Most children and adults are convinced that the word 'sweet' was there on the word list as in their minds, they associate all the words related to sweet taste. This 'false' memory was created when the mind associates words such as lolly, honey, sugar, pastry, cookie, pie, tart with the 'taste'—sweet!

Quiet Time!

Players: 2 to 3

Getting Ready:

Choose a time of the day when there is not much disturbance in the environment.

How to Play:

Maintain silence. Invite the child to listen to the sounds in the environment carefully.

Resources Required:
1. Unlimited quality time
2. Silence

Tickle the Thoughts:

1. Ask the child what they can hear.
2. Ask them why they were not able to hear the sounds before.

Goals Achieved:

- Concentration
- Listening skills
- Sound recognition
- Mimicry

TICK-TACK TIPS

1. During the activity, explain the importance of 'quiet time' to the child.
2. Visit a library and explain the importance of 'quiet time' to the child.
3. On the way to the school, encourage them to listen to various sounds.
4. Take the child to various places such as zoo, musical instruments shop, railway stations, and airport and ask them if they can imitate the sounds they had heard.

Conclusion

For a person, all that exists is 'memory' and without 'memory', the very existence of a person becomes immaterial. A child is born with a substantial capacity programmed into them by birth. An infant can recognize the mother by the fragrance of her body, which is an indication that a child has memory programmed into them.

But what happens to the memory as the child grows? Does the memory buckle under academic pressure?

Memory is the primary skill that needs to be trained from the time a child is born. Learning a sport, academics or life skills should 'not' be the primary focus in educational institutes. If a child cannot recall and reformulate the information, the purpose of going to the educational institute gets defeated!

To enhance productivity in any sphere of life, 'working memory' should constitute a part of the school's curriculum. Just as any other subject, working memory should be exercised from the beginning at the grassroot level, i.e., pre-school and then through high school, college and also at the workplace. As parents or facilitators who are aware, we will then be able to help the child to enhance the inner potentials that he or she has. Then, and only then, we can create and establish an empowered society—one that will expand its horizons of intelligence with 'sensitivity', where children will be the fountainheads of strength, inner peace and contentment.

Acknowledgements

I would like to thank my immediate family for stepping up and standing in for me while I would engage myself and put pen to paper.

The creative process of writing a non-fiction book is immensely intense and can intermittently be a very isolated journey. However, having encouraging friends when the going gets tough is a precious boon! I thank my friends for being a constant source of strength.

My sincere thanks to Shambhu Sahu and Yamini Chowdhury for their kind support. I thank Amrita Chakravorty for designing the cover of this book, Anurupa Sen for editing and Saswati Bora for giving her inputs and all others at Rupa Publications for investing time and effort in shaping the book to its present form.

To acknowledge is to express my gratitude to all of you who remain an integral part of my extraordinary journey. It is for you that this book became a reality.